SELECT ENDORSEMENTS FOR FRED DAWKINS
THE ENTREPRENEURIAL EDGE NON-FICTION SERIES (DUNDURN PRESS)

BOOK ONE: EVERYDAY ENTREPRENEUR: MAKING IT HAPPEN

"Fred Dawkins has written a wonderful book about entrepreneurship unlike any other in the market. He brilliantly uses his storytelling skills to illuminate his subject in a way that makes the book a joy to read. You're so wrapped up in the story that you may not realize how much you're learning until you've turned that last page."
—Terry Fallis, award-winning author of *The Best Laid Plans*, *Up and Down*, and others

"Fred Dawkins's easy-to-read writing style belies the critical importance of his subject matter, including a complex set of essential entrepreneurial skills and the important role of entrepreneurship in the global economy."
—Dr. Ajay Agrawal, Peter Munk Professor of Entrepreneurship at the Rotman School of Management, University of Toronto, founder of the Creative Destruction Lab, and presented with the Order of Canada 2022

"Fred Dawkins has pulled together a wealth of knowledge and advice crucial to the successful entrepreneur in a highly readable fashion. It is a must-read for aspiring and seasoned entrepreneurs who are facing today's complex, volatile, and uncertain world."
—Dr. Sherry Cooper, former executive VP and chief economist at BMO Financial Group

BOOK TWO: FAMILY ENTREPRENEUR: EASIER SAID THAN DONE

"In the age of Twitter, it warms the heart that 'smallbizpreneurs' still rule the roost and family business remains the proven formula."
—Peter C. Newman, legendary Canadian journalist and broadcaster

"This second book in the series ought to become the bible for every entrepreneur and budding entrepreneur as it is full of very valuable, helpful, and vital advice. Very cleverly written."
—Frank Weisinger, past national president of the Life Insurance Association (UK)

"Dawkins provides sage advice for anyone in a family business, emphasising how important it is to face the issues head-on as rationally as you can and not allow emotion to dominate. The valuable insights will guide you no matter where you are on the entrepreneurial time table."
—Dr. Elizabeth Stone, dean of The Ontario Veterinary College, University of Guelph

BOOK THREE: AGELESS ENTREPRENEUR: NEVER TOO EARLY, NEVER TOO LATE

"Entrepreneurship is not just for the young. It is a mindset and it's never too late to take charge of your life and become an entrepreneur. That is Fred Dawkins's message in a nutshell and nobody tells the story better of how to make the leap successfully. Fred's common-sense wisdom and experience shines through this journey of transformation—an excellent read for young and old and everyone in between."
—Tiff Macklem, Governor of the Bank of Canada

"The lessons you remember are the ones from good storytellers and Fred Dawkins is one of the best. I found myself nodding my head and smiling as I read *Ageless Entrepreneur*."
—David Tsubouchi, former Ontario Minister of Consumer and Commercial Relations

MY CAMINO

MY CAMINO

Things I Learned Walking With Our Grandson

FRED DAWKINS

Copyright © 2025 by Fred Dawkins
Interior Design by Daniel Pyle
Edited by Heather Sangster strongfinish.net

All rights reserved. This book or any portion thereof may not be reproduced or used in any manner whatsoever without the express written permission of the publisher except in the case of brief quotations embodied in a book review.

ISBN: 978-0-9877965-6-1

Published by Binkley & McLeod Publishers

This very personal memoir is dedicated to our six grandchildren, Jacob, Gareth, Elias, Hannah, Zina and Owen.

This narrative reflects everything that Nana and I have strived to achieve in building relationships with each and every one of you from memorable days at the cottage, to great family visits to Florida, to Nana days and sleepovers at our home. Reading stories together and making up stories like the Whopper series. All of these things involve the art of making memories resting firmly on the foundation of unconditional love. After this, I promise each of you a personal memoir of my life to share experiences and insight to read at times and to pass on to future family members.

A society grows great when old men plant trees in whose shade they shall never sit.
—Aristotle

I'm sure Aristotle did not foresee a group of old men driving around in a pickup truck, shovels in hand, placing saplings. Instead, I believe he meant planting the seeds of wisdom and experiences from a life well lived. I can only imagine a great, great grandchild of mine reading some of my thoughts in seventy-five years which help solve a problem. What a legacy.

The message to readers is to build relationships in the here and now. Work at it. But remember: it has never been easier to write a book and self publish it. Write about your life for your family. These things make for a meaningful legacy.

PROLOGUE

Much of what you read about the Camino makes it sound like very serious business, a medieval-style pilgrimage fraught with appropriate suffering and contrition. Most of the books written about "the Way" focus on the profound change that results from making the effort, whether that be mental, spiritual, or physical. Or they dwell on the preparation you'll need to do and the problems you'll encounter.

Well, my story is of a different journey, one that's grounded in humour and quirky observations. If you can't laugh at yourself and your circumstances, you will miss many of the lessons of this unique life experience. My Camino was a joyous event, awash in good fellowship, good food, beautiful scenery, friendly local people, old-fashioned fatigue from accomplishing daily physical goals, historical sites, and most of all the companionship of my grandson for the better part of six weeks. How lucky am I? At seventy-one, I proved that I could walk the eight hundred kilometres—not insignificant. But an even greater accomplishment was spending more than a thousand quality hours with my grandson. And, of course, we walked every single step because that's what twenty-two-year-olds do.

To be sure, there is a serious side to the Camino adventure. There is no denying that walking the Camino de Santiago constitutes an intimate personal experience. My Camino will be quite different from yours. The differences start with your purpose when you begin and end with your perception at the completion of the trek. For many, the undertaking is motivated by deeply entrenched religious beliefs and a desire to recreate a challenge attempted by so many others on a route of pilgrimage going back more than a thousand years. That's the Camino heritage. Arguably, this journey even predates Christianity and goes back to pagan times. Historically, a pilgrimage meant sacrifice, including hunger, danger, pain, and exhaustion—all an essential part of proving one's devotion to God. Only about forty percent of those walking the Camino today do so for religious reasons.

For others, the journey is spiritual in nature, an attempt to embrace the human spirit outside the defined parameters of organized religions. Everyone who walks the Camino has a personal reason for doing so. Some are seeking redemption. Some want to punish themselves. Most are seeking change or clarification of who they are or what they should do. For many it's simply facing the physical challenge. Regardless, sacrifice is still an integral part and essential for the sense of accomplishment that comes by completing the walk and receiving your Compostela (the certificate you receive for walking the Camino).

Sacrifice can take many forms. When you're twenty-two, dealing with Wi-Fi that sucks can be painful. But to a seventy-one-year-old, the relentless quest for effective Wi-Fi at every café and albergue becomes a daily joke (if you're wise as rumoured at your age, you keep that one to yourself). When you're seventy-one, every steep uphill or downhill you face represents pain. When you're twenty-two, that same terrain is just a welcome challenge. Running up those hills with a fifty-pound pack is a great way to motivate your grandfather—NOT REALLY!

Maybe the age difference blended our needs and abilities, producing humour that didn't exist for others. Maybe we didn't have a grandiose reason for walking the Camino. Actually, I did have a pretty meaningful motive: to create an unforgettable memory for my grandson.

Both of my grandfathers died before I was born. I have no memories of them—just a few faded pictures with muted explanations given by my parents, mostly confused by me or forgotten. Well, with more than eight hundred photos and numerous personal stories, Jacob will not face that dilemma. That video he took without me realizing it—catching me three-quarters of the way down a steep rocky path that took over three hours to complete and uttering the fateful words "I've had enough of this shit. I need to find something different," or something to that effect—makes him laugh uproariously today and it will forever more. He will never forget that look on my face or the delight he felt in cleverly recording me on video, and neither will I.

1
DECISION MADE

How could this have happened? How did I, a seventy-plus-year-old retiree, consider walking eight hundred kilometres in Spain, when a few short months before it had never entered my mind? I hadn't even heard of the Camino. I was no couch potato but was quite content walking on my treadmill three days a week for half an hour, followed by a ten-minute soak in the hot tub at the recreation centre in my retirement complex. That local scenery was all I needed. It reminded me of the Roman baths—exotic enough at my age and stage. Was it an urge to travel, like many retirees? No, I'd had my fill of that during my forty-seven years as an entrepreneur, visiting over thirty countries and more than forty American states. Besides, I was busy writing books and checking off items on my bucket list. Life was good. If anything, there wasn't enough time to do everything I had in mind. The very suggestion of abandoning my fully engaged extended middle age (old age doesn't exist) was preposterous.

Well, for starters, let me warn you. If anyone suggests watching the film *The Way*—starring Martin Sheen and his son Emilio Estevez, who also directed it—don't do it. Almost half of the people I met walking the route had seen the movie, and for many it was their first introduction to the Camino. The movie is pure bait, hooking many new pilgrims.

Second, don't watch it with one of your grandchildren, especially one who is in great physical shape and thrives on any challenge he encounters, going out of his way to take on things that few people his age, never mind mine, would even contemplate.

Just kidding, *sort of*; the movie is a compelling story and it gives you just enough of a taste of the Camino to catch your interest. It doesn't tell you everything (more on that later), but it does challenge you. As the credits scroll, your brain starts to race. *Could I do that? Should I do that?* Your inner self warms to the idea while your knees and feet begin to cringe. You can feel a tiny knot in your stomach tightening. Your throat is a little dry. When you look across the room, your wife has an incredulous expression and you can almost hear her thoughts, which are clearly: *You wouldn't, would you?*

The credits continue to scroll. You are definitely in a confused state, where your imagination magnifies both your ability and your thirst for adventure. Then you make the mistake of looking right into the eyes of your grandson Jacob. *Wouldn't it be great to share an adventure like that with him? Nobody gets that opportunity!* Lacking a defence mechanism and abandoning the instinct to protect your aging body, without any hesitation you utter the fateful words: "I'm in if you are?" One second later your fate has been sealed by his "I'm in." Two words, just three different letters, he hadn't even said he was interested. It will forever be "your" idea. Not really. Our minds were totally in sync. I just said it first.

That was in December 2015. We agreed to go the following September, right after Jacob completed his contract for tree planting in northern Ontario. We all know how flighty kids are today. He would almost certainly pull out once he realized the downside of hanging out with someone almost fifty years older for six full weeks, right? No millennial could endure that; I mean, seriously, with the current pace of change, the generation gap between grandparents and grandkids is impossible.

For six months with occasional reassurance from my wife that nobody but her could tolerate me for six weeks, I waited for him to cancel. Then panic set in and I started to train in earnest. In my heart I knew that Jacob was not a quitter, and for that reason alone I couldn't quit either. After writing three books on entrepreneurship, my mindset dictated what would happen. Jacob finishes what he starts and so do I. That is what entrepreneurs do in business and in life. So that's how I found myself on a bus going from Pamplona to Saint-Jean-Pied-de-Port on September 21, 2016, gasping at every hairpin turn in anticipation of walking back.

2
WHAT IS THE CAMINO?

The full name of the pilgrimage is El Camino de Santiago de Compostela. The Spanish word *camino* can be translated as "path or road, route or journey." *Iago* is the Spanish form of "James," while *sant* means "saint." In other words, to be precise, in English we're dealing with the Way of St. James. Significant to our story, the Hebrew name from which the anglicized James derives is Jacob. This means I walked the Way of Saint Jacob with my grandson, whose name happens to be Jacob. An interesting coincidence. But who was St. James, and why is he the patron saint of Spain?

His quite legitimate claim to fame is as one of the twelve apostles, significantly one of the first disciples along with his brother, John, and Peter to join Jesus and rumoured to be the second one to die, after the infamous Judas Iscariot. He has a number of names, including James the son of Zebedee, Saint James the Great, Saint James the Greater, Saint James the Elder, and Saint Jacob of Santiago. That name Jacob keeps coming up. The adjectives *elder* or *greater* are applied because of a second apostle named James the Less, who was apparently younger and shorter. Our James was known to have a fiery temper. Reputedly, King Herod had him executed. I refer you to the New Testament for more information. Regardless, what does this have to do with Spain?

James's special status as the country's patron saint derives from the Legend of St. James (*Sancti Jacobi* in Latin), which affirms that around 40 AD he was preaching the Gospel in Hispania before returning to Judea, where he was beheaded on the order of Herod. With the help of angels, his decapitated body was removed to Spain, arriving in an unattended boat. There are different versions of how this was accomplished, but the essence of the legend is that his remains arrived in Spain. What happened next is complicated (and material for you to research if you like), but for our purposes the belief is that his remains were hidden in Spain until the ninth century, when like a number of Christian relics they were discovered. There are stories of his reappearing as a medieval knight, the patron and protector of Spain. His symbol is the scallop shell bearing the red cross of St. James. The French term *coquille St. Jacques* stems from that. Regardless of these folklores, his remains now reside in the Cathedral at Santiago de Compostela, consecrated in 1211, a place of pilgrimage since the Middle Ages. It was promoted by the Spanish as one of the most holy places in Europe, ranking close to Rome and Jerusalem as one of the great destinations of the time. It was also more accessible to western Europe than the other two, particularly during the occupation of parts of Europe by the Moors.

That is a very short summary of the very long history of pilgrimage to the sight which established the exalted position that our end destination has held for more than a millennium. More about the modern Camino to follow after some details about my personal journey.

3
YOUNG MAN WITH A HORN

My Camino was different than most, driven by the desire to build an adult relationship with my grandson. Jacob is our eldest grandchild, the oldest of five, having two brothers and two sisters with just one cousin on our side of his family but seven on the other. Birth order has a major impact on every family dynamic, arguably cutting carefree youth prematurely for the oldest and causing challenges for which none of us are prepared at a young age. Being the youngest or in the middle brings a completely different set of issues. I worry about all my grandchildren but, as the first, Jacob introduced me to many new possibilities in a rapidly changing world.

Like most of us are in our early twenties, Jacob was in the midst of figuring out life, a little confused and occasionally misdirected. Like any self-respecting grandfather, albeit with limited experience in that role, I wanted to help him get onto a solid life path. As we set out on this unique adventure, my hope was to build an unbreakable bond between generations separated by five decades. I suppose this was literally the initial step in seeking that type of connection with all six of my grandchildren, magnified by the reality that this was an opportunity I'd been denied due to the premature death of my grandfathers.

Jacob was born when I was forty-eight. Arguably my first fifty years brought about more change than any comparable period in history. World population moved from two billion to eight billion. The Soviet Union peaked and collapsed. Life expectancy improved. In the west, religion declined. So much more had happened. Jacob's first twenty years were far different than mine, exposed to virtually everything and insulated from very little. What better way to know each other, warts and all, than spending almost every minute of six weeks together in the midst of a demanding physical challenge, at least for me. But how would this intergenerational relationship evolve? What if our needs and likes just didn't mesh? Well, it turns out that the Camino is a great equalizer, highlighted by the isolation from so many distractions that preoccupy us day by day. What I learned went far beyond the countless interactions between us.

Each person's Camino really is unique to them. Part of that difference stems from the people who you meet along the Way. Generally, you fade in and out with a dynamic group of *peregrinos* (Spanish for "pilgrim") who start as much as two days ahead of you or two days behind. Some pull ahead only to drop back. Others you never see again. Some just pass you by or you pass by them, but many move at a similar pace. It's a fluid group within which you see people along the trail or at cafés or albergues (the dormitories, pronounced *al-bear-gays*) off and on, sometimes within hours, days, or even weeks. Within that moving subset of pilgrims, a few people will stand out. Maybe it's because of their appearance or personality or intellect or often for their kindness, but you *will* notice them and you'll definitely remember them.

Within our travelling entourage, my grandson was one of the "memorables." That distinction should have been obvious from the beginning when Jacob arrived at our door the afternoon we were leaving for Spain. I had been struggling for weeks to reduce the weight of my backpack, eventually shrinking it down to about twenty-six pounds. As I found out later, that was still far too much. That is too much for almost everyone but Jacob, who arrived with a fifty-pound pack plus a newly purchased, slightly used saxophone in a separate case. I'd completely forgotten that he'd played the sax for one year in high school several years before. Whatever the reason, he felt this was a much-needed diversion along the trail. I will never understand why he needed it, but the sax definitely played a distinctive role in our tale.

My wife Karin's reaction was instant and quite logical. "Don't you think a harmonica is more appropriate?" Maybe so, but we all know that the concept of what's appropriate or not is fairly subjective. If you do decide to walk the Camino, there are no limits beyond your ability to carry whatever you decide is suitable. You will undoubtedly overshoot the mark, but it will be your decision. For Jake, that meant a ten-pound saxophone and a lot more *and* he could handle it. My selfish reaction at the time, which I managed to keep to myself, was *Oh no, how will he be able to carry some of my things if I need help?* Of course that had always been my fallback plan: dear old Gramps might just need some help from his much younger, stronger, and faster grandson. I shouldn't have worried. No matter how much he was carrying, Jacob was ready to help me if I struggled in any way.

He also arrived wearing his favourite tree-planting shirt: flamboyant, flowery, noteworthy, not outrageous but definitely noticeable. Had you met us along the Way, you would have come to know this handsome young man in his colourful shirt, wearing a large, heavy backpack and carrying a saxophone, playing it from time to time, and travelling with his grandfather, which was unusual in itself. Did I mention that he also had a very healthy prominent dappled beard? So, would you have remembered him?

I'm pretty sure the answer is yes.

The key words here are *come to know* because that's the most important thing I was hoping for on my Camino. There is much more to tell, but what I found early on was a young man eager to try his Spanish, which pleased the local merchants to no end, often leading to praise for his efforts and a bigger piece of chorizo. A polite, thoughtful, and unique personality who related to others of any age, always willing to offer a helping hand, being neither saint nor sinner. All that in the first

few days. But I was on the verge of the opportunity to know my grandson in a way that I suspect very few grandparents get to do. That was my mission. Anything else that might come out of my Camino would be pure gravy—and as it turned out, there was plenty of it, both figuratively and literally.

4
THE MODERN CAMINO

The Reformation and numerous wars in Europe caused the decline of the original pilgrimage. For a long period, the route was largely ignored, but in the early 1970s a small group initiated a revival that has snowballed and continues to build momentum. Since the year 2000, almost four million people have traversed all or part of the Camino in different ways. It has lifted the economy of northwest Spain due to its matchless version of tourism and camaraderie. In 2024, an estimated 450,000 people will have walked, biked, rode horses, or bussed some part of the Camino. Reflective of the fact that medieval pilgrims came from all over western Europe, several routes reach the final destination at the cathedral, including the French Way, the English Way, the Portuguese Way, the Camino Primitivo, and the Camino del Norte, to name but a few. The most common one, which we followed, is the Camino Frances, beginning at the town of Saint-Jean-Pied-de-Port in the foothills of the Pyrenees in southern France. Although there are four branches from various starting points in northern France leading to Saint-Jean (making for much longer routes), this quaint community in the Basque region is the designated starting point for the current eight-hundred-kilometre adventure that the majority of modern-day *peregrinos* experience.

Jacob and I started on our trip together on September 21, 2016, leaving the house in Guelph, Ontario, around 3:00 p.m. to go to Toronto Pearson International Airport. We arrived in Saint-Jean-Pied-de-Port twenty-three hours later, after flying first to Dublin, then to Barcelona, and taking the train to Pamplona, followed by a bus to Saint-Jean, all arranged via the Internet with the transfers made smoothly but not without incident. Life's little comedies played out along the way. Jacob forgot his new watch and new hat on the first flight. By the time he realized it, there was no time to go back through customs and try to find them. He was not in a good mood and this was a poor start, which didn't get better.

When we arrived in Barcelona, his fifty-pound backpack didn't arrive. He had checked the pack as is, clearly recognizable. My more modest pack was shoved into a larger black bag that looked like any other duffle and gave no hint of our purpose. Differences in our age-related priorities were emerging. Of course, Jacob had packed his bag the morning before we left. He wasn't concerned about the weight. Why would he be?

At this point, significant doubt was creeping in concerning just how well we would be able to relate. Edgy old dude versus happy-go-lucky young guy. After much consternation on my part, and a little frustration due to our limited Spanish, we understood that the pack might arrive in Barcelona the next day. Not much help. Eventually we arranged to have the pack transferred to the airport in Pamplona, where we were supposed to be after walking for four days. My travelling companion was unphased. So off we went with Jacob having no change of clothes, no jacket, no soap, no shampoo, no water bottle, no comfortable footwear for the evening, basically zero essentials *but* he did have his sax. Fortunately, we just made our train to Pamplona and were able to catch our bus to Saint-Jean-Pied-de Port. We got to our bread and breakfast, called La Maison Ziberoa, just before dusk. Jacob ran out and found a pizza, which we gobbled down before falling into bed. We wisely got up when called for breakfast and immediately started off on our eight-hundred-kilometre walk.

If you're not sure, the term *wisely* was sarcasm. It was not wise at all. So, my first advice for you: allow at least one extra day in Saint-Jean to acclimatize before you rush into your Camino! Now, back to things that I learned.

5
A SANDWICH IS NOT ALWAYS A SANDWICH

Before we left for Spain, Jacob and I had managed to cram in some Spanish lessons. I tried the interactive Pimsleur program (which I recommend), while Jake was happy using his phone and an app called Duolingo. Both approaches were more than adequate and if you take your phone, which you will, Duolingo comes in handy. If you decide to walk the Camino, you need to learn some Spanish because very little English is spoken in some of the villages. Stick to the basics. Believe me, you'll get over your inhibitions quickly when you need food or a place to sleep. You will always be hungry so be able to order simple breakfasts, lunches, and dinners, plus ask for a room, definitely potable drinking water, and possibly a bathroom and not too much more. You could stumble along without trying, but it's much more fun to try and the locals are very friendly and helpful, even when you mispronounce words, which you will. Spanish has some different pronunciations that are awkward at first.

Along the way you will encounter a pretty steady diet of chorizo (sausage), tortillas (omelettes), bocadillos (sandwiches), as well as three-course *peregrino* menus in the evening with plenty of local wine. The choice with your meal each night is between water (which you really need) and wine (which you really want). The latter flows just like the water, but it's generally a light table wine that probably won't cause a hangover. At least I managed to avoid any after-effects, but you definitely don't want any when you're facing a twenty-five-kilometre walk with plenty of ups and downs the next morning. Regardless, I arrived in Spain confident that I could request what I needed, relying on my newfound language skills to ensure that I could order a nice sandwich for lunch.

However, I learned very quickly that bocadillo doesn't really mean sandwich, even if Duolingo says so. Oh, the basic components are there, but what it really means is a half-loaf of bread sliced, with nearly a pound of cheese inserted. It costs about three euros. The bread is actually a Spanish baguette, which is at least twice as big as we see in Canada. I mean it; this sandwich uses the entire oversized baguette and it may not be quite a pound of cheese but it seems like it. In every village you will see the locals marching home with these baguettes daily, sometimes carrying two or three. It's a mainstay and you'll always get extra bread whatever you order, no matter how unlikely the combination. There seems to be small bakeries in every village, town, and city.

Naturally, Jake could eat a bocadillo and a tortilla and a chorizo for lunch no problem, and that was after the three breakfasts we had most mornings. The joys of being twenty-two on holiday (sort of) and surrounded by cheap food. I was lucky if I could eat half of my bocadillo. We estimated that he out-ate me about four to one on the trip and that's conservative. Anyway, I also learned quickly that if asked for onions (*cebollo*) and tomato (*tomate*) along with the cheese, my bocadillo was much tastier and they would make it up fresh. I also learned to ask for my omelette *calor* (heated) and my water *frio* (cold). Cold omelettes and warm water just don't work for me, but you'll get them if you don't ask. More food stories to follow.

6
IRISH MILES ARE SMILING

You can expect the first days of your Camino to be the most challenging physically. At night you're sure to be exhausted, starving, but full of this new experience while meeting a wide range of people of different ages, body types, nationalities, and opinions. Stories will be flying and the wine flowing because adrenalin is high and no one is quite tired enough to skip the wine yet. People will be wandering in late to cheers of encouragement because everyone is finding their own pace while adjusting their conditioning to this new reality. There will be a lot of whispered speculation about who won't make it all of the way. Most do. The farther you get, the more determined you become. All of this tends to equal out over the first two weeks, not that a seventy-one-year-old ever comes close to keeping up with his twenty-two-year-old compatriot who, thank goodness, had the patience of Job to go at my speed most of the time and wait for me to catch up the rest of the time. It was just great to see him waiting for me patiently at the top of a ten-degree slope only to stand up as soon as I got there and say, "Well, let's get going." He actually only did that a few times and his claims of my profane responses are greatly exaggerated.

One of my favourite moments was the second or third night out when we met three Irish ladies, all in their sixties, who had started the day before we had. When we asked them how they were finding things, they said, "Really tough. These Spanish kilometres are a lot longer than the ones we have in Ireland." They were bewildered when we laughed. We thought they were kidding, just showing the renowned Irish sense of humour, but they were serious.

"No, we've been walking for weeks in Ireland to get ready and the kilometres here are much longer. It takes forever." They were adamant and wouldn't listen to our insistence that all kilometres were the same distance no matter what the country, even if the terrain was something else. We saw them almost every night for the first week and always asked how they were finding the Spanish kilometres. They never wavered from their fervent belief.

At the end of the first week, they announced they were heading home and would be back next year to do another week. That was the first time I realized that a lot of Europeans break up their Camino over several years (more on that form of underhanded pilgrimage later). As I trekked on, I often thought of the three Irish ladies with their beer in hand and a twinkle in their eye, insisting that Irish kilometres were much shorter. Without fail, the thought always brought a smile to my face and made my day a little easier. It still does.

7
THE COUNTDOWN

One day during that first week, as we sat in the shade in a forested area, I started to laugh for no apparent reason. Jacob looked at me in wonder. Had the heat got to me? It hadn't, but I'd just found some humour in our new reality. He had spent all summer doing hard physical work tree planting to earn a relaxing holiday that now consisted of carrying a fifty-pound pack in extreme heat across fairly demanding terrain. Not that funny, but at the time I thought it was hilarious. Apparently, he agreed, because he started to laugh as well. That was the initial stir-crazy moment in one of those first demanding days, a tendency that I soon labelled "Camino Crazy." There would be many more instances of such shared silliness. Moments for which "you had to be there" to appreciate.

We quickly settled into the routine of the trail. The most daunting challenge of the night, as you lay on your bunk, mapping out your goal for the next day, was calculating the number of kilometres to the finish. Eight hundred kilometres had sounded demanding back at home, but after the first few days, seven hundred more seemed unreachable. Those first days, each night, the proverbial carrot in front of the donkey, seemed farther out of reach as you dragged your weary body into bed. Would that ever change? Finally, a quick look at your phone to stay somewhat in touch with the outside world and then lights out at ten. So simple—so demanding—but unexpectedly ever so satisfying!

8
A TALE OF STICKS AND STONES

Whenever I told anyone that I planned to walk the Camino, there was one of two responses. Either they said "Congratulations," which didn't seem at all fitting. I mean, if you finished fourth at the Olympics, most people would say something like "Oh, that's too bad." Nobody actually congratulates you for just showing up, and I hadn't even done that yet. Their kudos made me uncomfortable and I would quickly reply, "Oh, don't congratulate me unless I do it. When I reach Santiago de Compostela, you can send some praise my way, but not before." How embarrassing would it be after all this undeserved admiration to admit that I had to quit? For that reason alone, I stopped telling people that I was going. The second response was far more frank: "Why on earth would you want to do that to yourself? Do you know how far eight hundred kilometres is?" When I answered, "Sure, it's five hundred miles," the typical reply was: "That's even worse. You're crazy, you'll never do it!" I'm still not sure why it's worse, but most people seemed to think it was. Apparently more than our new Irish friends had a distorted sense of distance. Combining the threat of not making it with the understanding that most people didn't think I could do it anyway led to more than a few mind games right up to leaving. At that point it didn't matter because I was committed, or was it that I should have been committed? Anyway, telling me I wouldn't do it or that I could always take a bus kind of pissed me off. There was no turning back.

Naturally, I received lots of advice from those whom I did tell: people who would never do it, and never wanted to, but clearly knew how. Obviously, I needed help and who better to give it than some of my couch-potato friends. One often repeated suggestion was to make sure that I took walking sticks. My initial thought was *I'm in pretty good shape and I never use walking sticks on the treadmill. Why would I need them?* Fortunately, my wife insisted that I buy a set and try them. I even used them during my last week of preparation. They didn't seem that helpful on the flats around home. Reluctantly I had packed them. Let me tell you a few reasons why you will want them. On uneven ground, which there happens to be a lot of in Spain, they give you stability. On the steep uphill paths in the mountains, they allow you to use your arms to pull and your legs to push, à la Dr. Doolittle and his push-me-pull-you. Your legs will thank you, your arms not so much. But most of all you need your sticks on the downhill. For some reason I thought that the downhills would be easier—even a bit of a break—NOT! On a ten percent downslope, your toes will be shrieking. Your knees will be collapsing. Your brain will shut down. Screaming is very tempting as these downhills seem to last forever. If you use walking sticks, it's estimated they will bear up to twenty percent of your weight and literally take that much of the load off your knees. I'm sure that's why my knees held up so well.

I was such a perfect candidate to walk the Camino. There goes that sarcasm again. In the previous few years, I had ended my tennis days by tearing my meniscus, had pulled my Achilles tendon twice, and struggled from time to time with plantar fasciitis. In just a few years since, I have confirmed arthritis in both knees and both hips, with my left knee being bone on bone. With all of this, I wore orthotics so foot problems were likely, *but* my feet held up great. I'm sure that my sticks, along with my shoes and socks, were part of the reason. I spent a lot of time researching and choosing the right shoes and socks, for me: Keen Koven hiking shoes (not boots) and merino wool socks. I tried four different types of footwear on local trails before I settled on Keen Koven. Time well spent. But you have to find what's right for you.

There's more to the Camino than your own limitations. For instance, there are the stones that seem to cover Spain indiscriminately, but especially right on *your* particular path, on the downhill portion at the end of the day. They are definitely not your friends and you quickly get to hate them, no matter how interesting they may look. Trekking downhill at the beginning of your Camino will seem like walking down a dry (depending on the season, wet might even be worse) steep creek bed. Imagine that at the end of a long day for about two hours, as you're picking your way, trying to avoid a fall. Tough sledding, but you will feel great when you finish—and those sticks I mentioned? They will become extensions of your arms, saving you from falls or twisted ankles and your knees will certainly thank you. Treat your sticks with love because you won't want to do your Camino without them.

By the way, you will have some interesting conversations with various body parts as you make your trek and it pays to listen. Sound weird? Remember Camino Crazy. Six weeks of walking every day will create some peculiar moments, but more on that later.

9
BE PREPARED

Almost no one who goes on a whim, as many do, is fully prepared for what lies ahead in Spain. Anyone can do it, but how you do it and how much you enjoy it will be affected by your preparation. Remember the typical boot camp movie scenes that show every type of recruit arriving, from that very fat guy who can't climb a rope to the super-fit guy who outperforms everyone else, knows what's coming, and has been training? That range is exactly what you'll see on the first day of your Camino. Which one will you be?

In addition to the recommendation of walking sticks, I received a myriad of suggestions on how to prepare. Seriously, these people who "would never attempt the Camino" knew so many things that I should do to get ready. Some of the ideas gave me a false sense of confidence, like *How hard can it be if Martin Sheen just went cold turkey in* The Way?

Because of that movie, the prevailing attitude, including mine, seemed to be: *How hard can it be to walk twenty-two kilometres a day?* A few trial runs at home and away you'd go. But the Camino is not a walk in the park. It's hard, every day, day in and day out—only serious hikers will be ready and most pilgrims are novices. Walking twenty-plus kilometres once or twice a week does almost nothing. Various people will tell you to not overdo it, just walk regularly and build up gradually to the distances you'll be doing in Spain. My advice is simple: OVERDO IT! The only way to train for walking an average of twenty-two kilometres every day for five-plus weeks is to walk twenty-two kilometres every day for an extended period of time. And do bring your sense of humour, there will be many reasons to laugh, even at your own expense.

Then there's your pack. Most suggestions are to start carrying your pack the last week of training. Why wait? Don't! You'll be carrying that pack every day, so start early and in the process make sure it fits well and is comfortable. You will repeatedly read that you shouldn't carry more than ten percent of your body weight (unless you're like Jacob, then you can carry thirty percent or more). In contrast, you'll also receive tons of recommendations and read copious lists of items you *should* bring with you. Think about these recommendations carefully and decide what *you* must have. Then cut that list in half. The best advice is to be prepared to buy things you need once you actually need them. Remember, you'll be passing through villages and towns daily. There's not much in the villages other than cafés and the occasional albergue, but most towns have *farmacias* and *supermercados* so you can buy medical supplies and food. One small frustration is that most of these towns close up shop mid-afternoon for siesta so various stores don't re-open until after 5 p.m. You'll quickly get used to that minor inconvenience though—and that one-hour nap after a shower at the end of your walk for the day soon becomes a nice routine. I'm still doing it.

10
A FEW NOTES FROM OUR FIRST DAY

We were sent off that first day, September 22, by our very charming hostess, Marie Josée Lagord, from her delightful home operating as bed and breakfast: La Maison Ziberoa in Saint-Jean-Pied-de-Port (unfortunately now permanently closed). The building was a sturdy Basque dwelling, nicely renovated with a distinct cozy atmosphere, and a welcoming dining room with white-washed walls and chestnut flooring where her guests sat around a large oak table for a generous breakfast. After a long day of travel, I noticed none of this on arrival. My full appreciation that first evening consisted of a thirty minutes spent ravenously devouring a pizza in our room followed by tumbling into a very comfortable bed and sleeping soundly for ten hours. That first breakfast was the best and the most complete of the trip, partially because we could relax with a short day ahead. No rush to get on the trail.

At we sat round the table with five others, our hostess served up hot cereal, grapes, oranges, bananas, fresh bread, croissants, and several types of jam and much needed freshly brewed coffee. We were introduced to Richard from California, who was about my age, and two Australian teachers, Theresa and Kathy, who we would see off and on for the next five weeks. There were two other Australian ladies who were going home, skipping their planned pilgrimage because one had injured her leg. She was the first Camino casualty that we met. It was a surprisingly laidback morning. Everyone seemed hesitant to get started. Was that trepidation? After filling the table, our Marie Josée joined us, recounting some of her own experiences walking the Camino and made a few helpful suggestions. These recommendations from someone who had completed the Way were more meaningful than all the ill-advised ideas passed on by my friends at home. A little late but still beneficial.

Day 1 is the most difficult of the entire trip and *not* because it is Day 1. The distance is twenty-five kilometres but is rated as the equivalent to thirty-two when adjusted for the climb, which is more than a thousand metres. If you're so foolish to go at it in one day, the last two to three hours you'll be coming back down five hundred metres on a steep rock-filled slope with your knees screaming, your toes rubbing constantly on the front of your boots, in a state of dehydration because you should have filled up your water bottle and of course you're very tired. When the temperature is over thirty degrees Celsius as it was for us in late September, the experience might seem a little like climbing down into hell. Does that not seem like something a masochist would enjoy? The good news is that you will have passed through the Pyrenees from France into Spain, but you'll still be in a Basque region so you'll notice very little difference.

However, there is one and only one opportunity to avoid this long and difficult day. If you recall the film *The Way*, this is the day when Martin Sheen's character wanders into the albergue in Roncesvalles, well behind anyone else, relying on his headlamp to see the path. Definitely something you should avoid. Coincidentally, all of us at that first breakfast had received the same advice: break up that first day—thirty-two kilometres with a significant climb followed by an equally serious descent are too much to start. Our hostess confirmed that we were wise to stop at Orisson. That's why we were unperturbed. Much different than what lay ahead, being expelled from most albergues at seven-thirty every day without fail.

Optimism ruled the day as the five of us set out together to walk our first eight kilometres, literally easing into the journey. We didn't even leave until ten-thirty that morning, after Jacob and I went out and got our credentials, officially launching our journey by getting the first stamp (*sello*) on our passports. The first hour was blissful. It was a beautiful sunny day. I felt terrific and so happy to be starting out. After two hours of walking up a ten percent slope at close to thirty degrees Celsius (eighty-six Fahrenheit), I was dragging my butt and had accepted that my training, as seriously as I thought that I'd taken it, was totally inadequate. I was into on-the-job training and I had thirty-five more days and almost the full eight hundred kilometres to go. Mildly discouraging but not for Jacob, who was sailing along enjoying every minute. So much so that he carried my pack for the last hour while I carried the much lighter saxophone and he walked back, keeping company with Richard, who was really feeling the heat.

With the added boost of a lighter burden, I marched enthusiastically into Orisson, ecstatic that we had decided to stay there. By one o'clock, I was sitting in the café with an ice-cold Coke Zero in hand—only seven hundred and seventy kilometres to go! That's right, the full pilgrimage is about seven hundred and seventy-eight kilometres, but those of us who have walked the full distance like to round it off at eight hundred. To prove us wrong, you have to walk the entire way before deciding whether or not you agree (higher estimates will be seriously considered). Remember, there'll be a few detours along the way.

Jacob and I were ecstatic, as were most others we saw that day. We were on the Way! This didn't seem too bad, even for me. Our chatter was upbeat and spoke to our excitement of getting started. Although we had climbed up almost three thousand feet, this was starting out to be a breeze (definitely "misguided optimism"). I had a nice relaxing lunch with Richard overlooking the Pyrenees, highlighted by a herd of Charolais cattle walking right through the middle of the village. That was to become a common sight. Cattle were welcome in many of the villages.

And where was Jacob? Well, he had taken his newly acquired saxophone to a nearby ridge, found a beautiful place to sit under a tree overlooking the valley, and was sending some haunting, albeit somewhat disjointed, heartfelt sounds echoing across the valley for all the would-be pilgrims to hear. He was also wearing his noteworthy colourful shirt so that day alone cemented his notoriety within our Camino. Maybe everyone should carry a sax on the Camino? Not really, but having his sax did open up an interesting opportunity—more on that to come.

11
ORISSON, DEAR ORISSON

Orisson was very special, perhaps the most unique layover we had on the entire trip. That initial climb was demanding but it didn't last long. Just long enough to give you a slight sense of accomplishment and some misled confirmation that you were deep into the challenge of the Camino. But it was over quickly. It was the only day on the entire trip that we felt comfortable enjoying that leisurely lunch, secure in the knowledge that we didn't need to complete another eight or ten kilometres before we could relax at the end of the day.

The scenery was spectacular: overhanging the side of the mountain, the café deck looked out across the surrounding valley. A second glass of wine seemed in order as Richard and I, who were the oldest two that day, compared notes on our first few hours. Richard had struggled with the heat. He was grateful that Jacob had gone back to join him, describing him as "a nice young man," a compliment I heard numerous times over the next five weeks. I attempted to show some empathy and assured him that we had very few climbs that severe ahead and his conditioning would certainly improve, as would mine.

After that long-drawn-out lunch, I spent the afternoon stretched out on my bunk reading my Brierley guidebook to the Camino with new respect, studying what was ahead for the next three or four days. More on the importance of Brierley later. I also took advantage of the Wi-Fi to send out a few emails, bragging about how great it was to be up in the mountains and off to a promising start. Life was good.

The communal dinner that night was exceptional, perhaps the best night we would have on the entire trip, at least one of the more memorable. Not because the food was that great—it wasn't—but we were hungry and we were eager, full of pride that we were finally on the Camino. And not because the company was the best we would have, because it might not be. And definitely not because we had accomplished so much, because we hadn't.

The magic that night was that forty-five people, the largest group at any communal dinner we would have, were all in the same position. We were learning the ropes together. As dinner was being served, each of us had to stand and introduce ourselves. Some had already developed blisters. One couple, who appeared to be in their mid-fifties, both significantly overweight and obviously out of shape, had struggled to make that first innocuous walk. We never saw them again after that first night. I am quite sure they dropped out. What were they thinking? Regular shoes, super-heavy packs, and no preparation. We also met their antithesis: a Canadian couple named Fred and Karen from Peterborough (their names a notable coincidence since my wife's name is Karin). They had trained well and had walked for two months at home carrying their fully loaded packs, reducing them until they were satisfied. They faded in and out of our next five weeks and beyond—but that's also a story for later.

I saw Jacob in a new light that night as he interacted with so many people older than himself from so many different countries. He was deferential, polite, and full of humour as more than a few people asked about his shirt and his sax. Most were enthralled by his revelation when introducing himself that he was travelling with his grandfather. I loved their reaction to that because at first quite a number thought I was his father.

The group introduction revealed some of the basic ingredients of a Camino. One at a time we had stood and given our names, our home, and the reason we'd decided to walk the Way. Jacob and I had received a warm welcome from those we hadn't chatted with yet because, as I indicated, meeting a grandfather walking with his grandson who had already been noticed for his sax playing was anything but common. There was a surprising number walking on their own. The most common reason was the challenge to prove to themselves that they could do it. Religion was mentioned. Meditation was mentioned. Personal tragedy was mentioned. Every answer was different. I'm quite sure that some were not willing to share on that first night.

Of the forty-five people enjoying themselves, there were more than a dozen countries represented that night, with the Australians and then the Koreans having travelled the greatest distance. In our little dorm room of six, there was an American (Richard), a Swede (Johnny), a Dane, a French Canadian from Montreal, plus Jacob and me. There were also more women than men at the dinner, which is a fairly typical picture for the Camino. The Orisson dorm was also the only place where the sleeping quarters were separated by gender. As we were close to the border, perhaps that's a difference between France and Spain. All of the Spanish residences were co-ed. As much fun as we were having, all good things must end. On the Camino, early to bed is definitely wise. That night, as for many to come, lights were out at ten o'clock. The dinner broke up as people went to their bunks and organized for the morning.

Settling into my bunk to do a little reading and review the next day became my routine each evening, but getting to sleep that first night was a challenge, at least for me. It seemed that every half-hour someone was getting up to go to the bathroom. Later, I became oblivious to anyone else, but that night I was totally aware of every movement, every snore, and every kilometre to be faced the next morning. The challenge ahead had become tangible and daunting—both aspects were on my mind.

That night seemed endless until we finally got up at six for an early breakfast. Jacob was anxious to get moving so we were the first to leave. Once I confirmed that I was up for it, we were on our way. We walked for almost an hour in the dark, which I found unnerving because it would have been easy to miss a marker. The air was crisp and clean, a contrast from the heat of the previous day, and the silence was equally refreshing. We talked very little. I was focused on the trail and Jacob had his headphones on, listening to music. Fortunately, the path was straightforward that morning.

Around seven, our Swedish roommate Johnny passed us at a good pace. He was a seasoned hiker who was frustrated that his wife was sick and couldn't join him on their planned walk though Spain. About half an hour later, we caught up to him sitting off the path, eating a banana. In our conversation the night before, he'd said that he planned to walk forty kilometres a day and complete his Camino in twenty days. (Thirty-three is the recommended timeframe). Recognizing that we were unlikely to see him again, Jacob jumped on his phone and blared Chuck Berry's "Johnny B. Goode"—totally appropriate. Johnny loved it and we shared a good laugh. We never did see him again, but I'll never forget the joy on his face and the sound of his laughter when he heard the music. Music can make an otherwise insignificant event memorable. But where did that come from?

It turns out that one of Jake's tree-planting mentors, an "old guy" in his fifties, had played in a band and loved music from just about every era. He and Jacob spent hours listening to different artists. Quite a few Beatles songs were among Jacob's favourites—perfect for me to listen to, but also a real boost to conversation. When I was Jacob's age, the biggest debate of the time was who was the most talented Beatle: John or Paul. I'm a left-handed romantic so I gravitated toward Paul. Ultimately, the Lennon-McCartney differences broke up the greatest band in history and then John was shot and killed. Despite the generation gap, Jacob and I had found one of what proved to be many common bonds. Listening to Lennon's "Imagine' with Jake as we approached Spain that morning was simply surreal. There was no fanfare, markings, or regulation at the border. At least none that I noticed. To be honest, I'm not sure exactly when we entered the country that we would embrace over the next five weeks.

After we arrived in Roncesvalles at 12:30 p.m., it was quickly agreed that there was no need to walk in the dark so leaving first thing was replaced with the more civilized approach of sleeping a little longer. The really great thing that started that day was spending long hours alone on the trail together and enjoying the first of many detailed conversations broken up by the odd sax solo, which I actively encouraged because it meant a longer break. Who would have believed there were so many benefits to having a sax in your pack? Our chats covered a myriad of topics. Initially family, the tree-planting experience, and his plans to join his girlfriend in Australia as soon as we got home. Politics and sports were regulars. As the trip went on, the topics became more future-oriented, both his and the world at large, from AI to vertical farming and beyond. The scope of his interests was encouraging. I had no idea that Jake was into meditation, so I was encouraged to give it a shot. And of course we discussed our fellow pilgrims.

Another new experience that first afternoon in Spain was our first taste of some of the pseudo-pilgrims that one encounters on their Camino. By far the most annoying of these less-than-pure *peregrino* types are the bus tourists: people who don't walk even one step along the Way but are fascinated by those of us who do, echoing statements like: "Oh, I've found one, I've found one" followed by "Can I take your picture?" and ending with "I admire you so much, I could never do it." We ran into a whole busload that afternoon so for a few minutes their interest was relentless, but at that point on our second day, I kind of enjoyed the attention; not so much later on. Most important memory from that day: just over seven hundred and fifty kilometres to go—serious progress!

THE FIRST WEEK

12
ENSALADA, NO ATUN, PERO MAS HUEVOS, POR FAVOR

After that first week, other than a small detour to pick up Jacob's backpack at the airport in Pamplona, our routine was firmly established. We had to be out of our albergue by seven-thirty each morning. The rest of the day was walk, rest, eat, repeat, with interesting conversations interspersed with stops at cafés and walks with new companions met over the course of the day.

Our fast-paced digital world was left behind with no hesitation as the immediate challenges of the daily distance to be achieved and the blisters to be avoided dominated our concerns. Generally, there was a café every five or six kilometres but not always. We averaged about twenty-three kilometres a day. That last week of September was hot, with peak temperatures each day of more than thirty degrees Celsius. It was essential to carry enough water.

The most welcome part of the day was still the quick shower and a short nap before dinner, often joining other pilgrims to share the day's experience over a meal and a glass or two of wine. There was a heavy emphasis on water conservation so the showers were pre-programmed and the water stopped after about a minute or so. You had to be quick.

Next was to wash your underwear of the day and let it dry. Two pairs are all you will need, one to wear and a clean one for after your shower to sleep in and for the next day. Believe me, the practical benefit of a lightweight pack trumps most of your preconceived needs. Travel light! Travel light! Travel light!

There were so many happenings along our journey, some more humorous than others. It's difficult to convey a spontaneous event that results in uncontrolled laughter. How do you duplicate your state of mind or the visuals that trigger the humour? How do you reproduce the precise interaction of all the players who create the comedy? So much of the hilarity lies in being an active observer of the farce that life serves up when it's least expected.

Well, one of these impromptu incidents bordering on slapstick happened to us twelve days into the walk, when we had completed about a third. The countdown that night was maybe five hundred and twenty kilometres to go. We were tired and not even halfway there. By this point end-of-day exhaustion was the norm. Concern about the remaining distance was increasing. Familiarity with your fellow travellers had developed. Emotions were raw. All of these impacts played into our state of mind. It happened in the tiny village of Ages, about sixty people. You really had to be there to appreciate it, and naturally it involved both fatigue and food.

After a few days on the trail, you realize that the *peregrino* menus are pretty much standard: generally, three courses with a list of choices for each. Hope you like pasta, chicken, and salad. The first course always includes an *ensalada mixto* option, which is pretty good because the vegetables are fresh but it often contains chopped-up tuna (or *atun*), which I don't like, and hard-boiled eggs, which I do like. So, I would usually ask for no tuna and extra eggs—*no atun, pero mas huevos, por favor*.

On this particular night, we decided to eat at a tiny restaurant in what was so far the smallest village we'd stayed in. There was no choice of venues. As we entered the tiny restaurant with just a few tables crowded into the limited space, we met Tom from the UK, who had recently completed his PhD in economics, and Nora from the Netherlands, who was taking a short break from school to walk part of the Way. We had met them earlier along the path that day and walked together for a short while. Since there were only four tables available, they asked Jacob and me to join them. They had already ordered. When I put in my standard ensalada order asking for *no atun*, Nora, who was a vegetarian, realized she had forgotten to specify the same.

Too late. The owner/bartender/waiter was just bringing her salad to the table and he didn't speak or apparently understand any English. No problem; in stepped Jacob and I with total confidence in our facility in Spanish to save the day. Big mistake. The owner wasn't buying any changes, even when Jacob offered to take Nora's salad and have the owner bring her a corrected one. Whatever he thought we said raised his blood pressure and energized his actions. Not acceptable, or at least not understood. Unlike most of the Spaniards we'd met along the Way, he had no interest in trying to decipher our heartfelt attempt to explain things in his native tongue. We had all just walked twenty-five kilometres so the salad didn't seem like that big of a deal. While Jacob continued to try to explain, the pace picked up, bolstered by Tom, Nora, and me trying to outdo each other through sarcasm. A tired pilgrim's sense of humour can lead to loss of control. Your sombre reality easily converts to the ridiculous. Camino Crazy!

All the owner heard was our laughter, which stirred him up even more, as he stood before us, salad in hand. The more we tried to explain, the more he gestured and raised his voice. But it wasn't threatening. His actions had a Chaplin-like slapstick flair, unintended of course, as he repeated himself over and over, adding to the comedy as we perceived it. What followed was a further torrent of objections in a Spanish diatribe at a speed we had no chance of comprehending. Had he been speaking English it would have been far less funny, but by this time we were out of control. Jacob's continual reassurances only made us laugh more. Holding up his hands and saying, "Despacio" ("slowly") didn't help a bit. Whenever there was a brief lull in the dialogue, continued giggling from Nora, Tom, and finally the unflappable sage, me, the grandfather, made things worse as Jacob patiently persevered, determined to make this fellow understand that he would solve the problem.

You did have to be there. The harder Jacob tried, the more animated our host became and the louder was our laughter. The more we laughed, the more frustrated he became. The scene felt more and more like a bit from a Woody Allen movie, with increasing wisecracks from Tom and me. The final straw came when the cook appeared from the kitchen. It was an *I Love Lucy* moment, when you find yourself confronted by an unforeseen twist to the parody in front of you. In our case, she was a large domineering figure, wearing a bandanna and a dirty white apron with the most severe and disgusted look on her face you can imagine. *Scowl* hardly does that look justice. It was too late for restraint, even Jacob gave up. Just her appearance was enough to have us rolling on the floor. At that point, drama and comedy came into conflict and the absurdity won the day.

Fatigue will do that to you. At least she put an end to the owner's complaints; maybe she was his wife, but there was no doubt about who was in charge. Somehow, we managed to get through the rest of the dinner without further incident. However, we ended up in stitches again at the end of the night when Tom attempted to mimic the fertility statue on the bar, which had a penis the size of its torso, so exaggerated that Tom was using a wine bottle as a prop. Silly for sure, but the whole night was a great release from the demands of the trail. We closed the place down around 11 p.m., which was on the late side. Lights were already out in our albergue.

I felt a little guilty about our treatment of the owner when we showed up at seven the next morning and he was on duty to serve us breakfast. The four of us were much more subdued, exchanging brief greetings with him. There was no sign of the cook. He was working sixteen or seventeen hours a day and our little charades were undoubtedly the last thing he needed. Our weariness from walking long hours had translated into laughter. His equally long time in the café had made him impatient and angry. We've all been there. I'm sure a steady stream of *peregrinos* can do that to you. These long hours are typical at most owner-operated village cafés and bars. The owners have to cover all the bases and usually with a smile on their face and a helpful attitude that contributes to making the Camino such a special experience. At least the resurgence of this modern trek has created opportunity for some in these small villages, which are typically struggling to exist.

After a short sleep by all, things were very civil. We ate a hearty breakfast and upon parting gave our reluctant friend another good tip. He smiled and wished us a "Buen Camino." My only regret is that we hadn't videoed the entire scene the night before because it would have been a sure hit on YouTube.

13
MIERDA, CAGADA, O ESTIERCOL

Many of the areas you walk through in northwest Spain are farmlands. Small independent farmers seem to have survived in Spain much more than in North America, where farms have been consolidated into large holdings to stay competitive. That observation may be overstated, but that's the feeling you get as you trundle through farm country. Some of the large vineyards, particularly in La Rioja, are exceptions, but you can count on seeing cattle walking the streets in many of the villages, looking you in the eye, clearly wondering what you are doing on their turf.

Our first encounter of this kind was back in Orrison, still in France, when the boss cow, with her bell on, led a small heard of white Charolais cattle right past the café. I'm not sure if you've walked among Charolais, but they are pretty big and a little intimidating when you're in their midst. Get used to it; you'll see cows, bulls, pigs, goats, sheep, horses, donkeys, dogs, chickens, and roosters. Some of them constrained but often not, and they don't really care where they dump. Neither does anyone else. And you will smell them. You definitely will smell them. So clear warning: do not step in it!

I'm not sure of the right Spanish word but *mierda*, *cagada*, and *estiercol* are all alternatives for "excrement." Don't get me wrong, this isn't prevalent. It isn't obtrusive or offensive. It is just part of the landscape. An integral part of the unique experience of walking across a foreign country acquiring irreplaceable insight into day-to-day life as you pass through. It's also one reason that the albergues insist you leave your walking sticking and shoes at the entrance every night. If you wander off the beaten path, you're likely to find some of the human variety as well because over 250,000 people (estimated 450,000 in 2024) pass along that way every year and some of them just can't hold it.

Most of the time the farms and the animals are a welcome sight: bucolic, rustic, pastoral, rural, and, without fail, peaceful. You will also see some massive fortress-style constructions of hay bales stockpiled in the fields, literally about thirty feet and at least ten large bales high and maybe fifty bales wide and twenty-five deep. That's my guess from afar. If you're seventy-one years old, these stockpiles are a distinct phenomenon a few hundred yards off the path, interesting to look at from a distance. If you're twenty-two years old, they represent a challenge, one that has to be climbed. When you reach the top, you yell down, "Hey, Gramps, can you grab my phone from my backpack and get a picture of me up here." So, we have several pictures of Jacob surveying the horizon like the conquering hero. Right after he climbed it, three other twenty-somethings came along, including Tom, but none of them could get up there, only adding to the legend of Jacob on the Camino. I could almost hear my wife saying, "Get him down from there, don't you know they can collapse and he'll be trapped." But that was not to be, and the pictures high up on the hay fort are among the more than eight hundred we accumulated.

As for the animals, they added to the ambiance, to the feeling that you were in another era, another world, reverting back to basics and most of all liking those feelings. On the Camino, you must find "your way" both figuratively and literally. Removing yourself from the clutter, the speed, the hyperbole, the hoopla, and so many other distracting factors beyond your control allows for the clear-minded assessment of, in the vernacular, "whatever ails you."

It opens the way for you to appreciate that grandson you've been worrying about, whether that be about his choices or his future. You find that he's become a thoughtful young man who is extremely likeable.

The fellow who insists on speaking Spanish, poorly or not, in small villages where English is rarely spoken, receiving a smile and a larger portion in return. He enjoys meeting people, talking to complete strangers at will, and is well liked by all he meets. The boy who had little use for formal education has become the man who constantly researches online with a questioning mind, eager to learn in his chosen way. The boy who you once carried around has become the man who carries your pack and eases your burden whenever he can. Wonderful to have a grandson who helps, and it doesn't hurt that he's in great shape. Well worth the effort and I would have walked twice as far to learn what I learned about him.

ANIMALS OF OUR CAMINO

14
THE BIBLE OF THE CAMINO DE SANTIAGO

You might think from the title that I'm talking about a holy book that includes details about St. James the apostle. You might feel that I'm about to turn religious on you and elaborate about some born-again experience that came over me while I was on "the Way." Sorry to disappoint.

While the book I have in mind will absolutely guide you through a small portion of your existence, one that could possibly result in changes to your life, it is not scripture in the biblical sense. However, it is an extremely practical, essential book. It's time that I introduced you to the late John Brierley. If you decide to experience the Camino, John will become your favourite author. No one has demonstrated more enthusiasm for this modern-day pilgrimage than Mr. Brierley. He updated his manual every year from 2004 to 2023 with a new edition, reliably current, until his passing. The result translates his passion and provides encouragement when you need it—and you will need it. You *must* read his book religiously before you go, as well as every night on your journey, and then afterwards to sustain your memories. It seemed to me that almost everyone carried a copy John's *A Pilgrim's Guide to the Camino de Santiago*. Trust me, buy one.

By the time you finish your personal trek, pages will be curled, maybe a few torn out (I wouldn't), but you will cherish it. This book, and the journal you *must* keep, offer the key to your memories of a unique period of your life. The Camino Blues are a real phenomenon, a form of withdrawal that I'll discuss later, but these two sources will help you recapture the essence of your Camino, a feeling only those who do this walk can know. Such mindsets are deeply personal and far from homogenous with others. If you're able to commit to the six weeks required to complete the full eight hundred kilometres, the mystique of the Camino can become an obsession. Rekindling those feelings is cathartic.

Back to Brierley. This is one of the most detailed, useful guidebooks I have every encountered. It breaks your adventure into thirty-three days. Some of you will take longer. Some will speedwalk faster. We broke two of the longer days up and took one full day off, so we were on the trail for thirty-six. Add three days in Santiago, two days of air travel, and a day in Barcelona, and that was our six weeks.

Each section of the guide is outlined in great detail using maps of the day, charts of the towns or cities ahead, including one by elevation for each day so you'll know the challenges you'll face. He explains some of the history, suggests articles to pack, outlines key phases in Spanish, and most of all creates enthusiasm for the path you'll follow. Each section includes every available albergue, every café where you can stop, every point of interest.

I studied Brierley faithfully. It was my bedtime reading. Jacob left that to me. It allowed me to plan the next day. How far we would go. What albergue we would target for the night. When we could break at a café. How much we would climb or descend. When and where we would encounter more difficult terrain. As the lights went out at ten, for a few minutes I would rehearse my day ahead until sleep took over.

In the morning, I woke up eager to get underway. As the day went on, I knew when I was within a kilometre of the much-needed next café or later on when my resting place for the night and the much-needed shower were close by. Brierley gave me a sense of direction in unknown territory whenever I needed it. Admittedly, on any given day I found that all kilometres were not the same. Don't tell the Irish ladies. Some days that last kilometre took forever. But when the last step was taken, I had hit my goal for that day. Simple. Satisfying. Simply satisfying. Hitting your goal every single day just feels good!

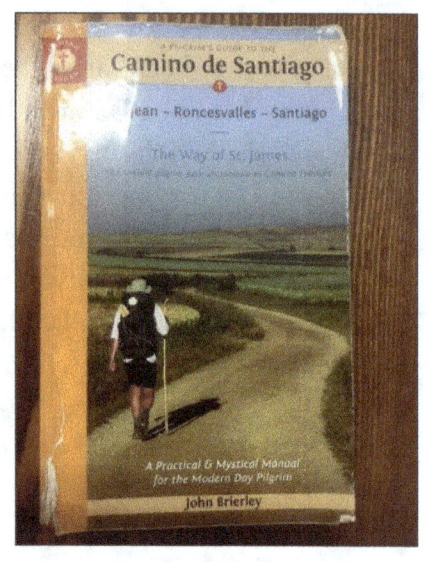

15
THE SOCIAL

T he Camino is an all-consuming exercise. It's also an enigma. So much time to think, but only one challenge to really focus on. Frankly, that was enough for me. It took my full commitment to just do it! For five full weeks my life was fixated on one thing: counting down those eight hundred kilometres. Lots of meaningful distractions but one dominant physical challenge, death by a million steps, actually renewal by a million steps. Whether you are there for religious reasons, spiritual reasons, the physical challenge, searching for answers, whatever, every day at some point you think about how far you have come and how far there's left to go. Signs posting the distance to Santiago are common, but when you see the mileage go up sometimes, as it does occasionally, and now you have thirty more kilometres to go than you thought you had the night before, you could just scream—and I did.

As an entrepreneur, I like to compare the challenge of the Camino to the first days of a start-up. It can be lonely; it requires focus and most of all determination. The task at hand is clear and success is within your control. In the first days, you don't know how to go about things. There is no passing the buck; no blaming others; no one else to march the steps. It is up to you and nobody else! But does it have to be?

Sounds pretty stark, especially if you're on your own, and it can be, but as solitary as the Camino sometimes seems, it's also a shared experience. Like so many start-ups, having a like-minded partner generates a special bond. Mine was with Jacob. But the partnership of the trail went well beyond that. For thirty-six days people faded in and out of our lives, all of us facing the same challenge, day after day getting up to walk yet again, the dormitories, the food choices, the varied terrain, the weather. When you're immersed in a challenge of your own choosing like this, everyone there is part of a mutual support group. Throughout, you share your experiences of the day and your plans for the next with people like Kathy and Teresa from Sydney, who we met on the first morning; Richard from southern California; Fred and Karen from Peterborough in Canada; Grace from Seoul; Ovietta from Avignon; Lorenz from Chambery, the four guys from Ulster; Marc and his father from Barcelona; France from Ottawa; Kim from Calgary; Michael from Prague, Tom from Nottingham, and so on, we were all immersed in this great experience for five weeks that went by quickly but lasted forever. For two days I walked on and off with Francisco from Barcelona, enjoying great conversations comparing the repeated attempts of Quebec to secede from Canada with the desire of the Catalonians to separate from Spain.

The Camino is a learning experience in a wide variety of ways. You learn about Spain and many other countries, but most of all you learn a lot about yourself and what you can accomplish. At seventy-one, you can and should surprise yourself. I certainly did. That's a critical life lesson that I emphasize in my writing on entrepreneurship. All of us have untapped capacities and when we really commit and dig deep, we are capable of far more than we realize. That critical recognition applies to physical challenges, work responsibilities, family obligations, and all relationships; virtually anything we want to accomplish. Mindset is the driving force that leads to results and achievement. Each of us is capable of simply making things happen. We can eliminate the word *if* from our vocabulary and focus completely on *how*, should we so choose. The Way of St. James is not easy, but anyone who really wants to do it can and will. The experience rebooted my determination and reminded me that anything is possible and that age is but a small hindrance if you choose to overcome it.

The lessons went on throughout the journey. Jacob was constantly getting tips from a number of Aussies on the trek because four days after we returned to Canada he was taking off for Australia. Kathy and Teresa arranged for him to meet them over Christmas in Sydney, and Kathy offered him the use of her home for three days. That's serious friendship arising from a special bond. Others are indelibly inked in my memory: Nicky, the girl from Liverpool who so wanted to play Jacob's sax and of course he let her, with her wailing forlorn attempt ending in a bout of shared laughter; Alfredo, a Spaniard living in Brussels who walked with a gaggle of four or five older ladies from various countries, sharing his extensive local knowledge; Fred and Marie from Salt Lake City who liked to walk holding hands; Ken from Saskatoon, who was on his third Camino so he focused on meeting new people; Antonio and Basia from Venice, whom we saw every day until they took the train to León and we lost them; Barb, a nurse from Portland who walked with us into Léon as we discussed the Trump phenomenon and American politics; Alex from Bulgaria, and so many more. There are dozens of other names I could add, people whose memories I share, entrenched in my journal and in my mind.

As time passes, the experience seems more and more like a fantasy. Did I really do that? The idea of walking eight hundred kilometres has become surreal. A dream so real, as it should be, but a reality that I know is fading as time goes by.

16
BACKTRACKING: GETTING TO GROUND ZERO

One night, maybe a week or so into the adventure, I reflected on how our journey had evolved. As you know, to get to Saint-Jean-Pied-de-Port, we had flown from Toronto to Dublin to Barcelona, then to Pamplona by train, and finally to Saint-Jean by bus. That part of the journey now seemed far in the past. Naturally, like the pair of twenty-two-year-old equivalents that I thought we were, we had got up and started walking the next morning. What was I thinking? Any allusion that I had totally recaptured my youth and was in great shape vanished that first morning. There was no way to hide that I'd become a man of my age, a phrase that only my doctor had used to describe me up to that point. But things were looking up. After that first week, I had moved forward from that wake-up call to some semblance of the much-needed conditioning required.

Quite literally, step by step, things continued to improve. I had shed weight daily and was well into my loss of twenty pounds. I was definitely tired every night and had found the heat oppressive, but now I was feeling my body changing. My mindset had changed. My perspective had changed. My relationship with Jacob was deepening day by day. Was all this the elixir of El Camino? I guess I'd drunk the Kool-Aid. All of this an ongoing process of adjustment.

Thinking back, I remembered that whatever discomfort I felt from that first long day of travelling was magnified on the trip from Pamplona. The bus was filled primarily with pilgrims, like us, and the first half-hour or so the mood was quite boisterous, buoyed by excited conversation. Once we were out of the city limits and started to go through the mountains, things quieted down. After the first series of hairpin turns around sharp corners from which the land fell off abruptly, you could feel a strong sense of apprehension as we collectively understood the commitment ahead. We were getting our first look at the terrain we would be walking. *Terrifying*: no other word does justice to the mood that evolved. That sense of confidence built up over two months walking varied lengths at home? It had evaporated in the first ten minutes of mountain driving. Trepidation had overwhelmed me. *We had to walk back over that area and return to Pamplona in three days?* In contrast, Jacob grinned at me in pure unadulterated excitement. Even though doubt was creeping in as the turns got sharper and the height increased, I reminded myself that I had done that distance and much more at home. Confidence was slowly trickling back. There was still a long way to go, but now I could and would do it! I had to do it! Jacob's smiling face demanded that I do it!

I had been mentally and physically exhausted those first few days. In other words, I was in a perfect (sarcasm again) state to tackle the eight-hundred-kilometre walk that first week. As for Jacob, we had already covered a lot of ground, literally and figuratively. Every day we had hours to talk but never exhausted our conversation. While I was asleep by 10:15 every night, he remained awake to use the Wi-Fi to connect with his girlfriend who was already in Australia and his friends back in Canada. The mode was firmly set; most nights would evolve with me asleep early and him staying up and staying connected. He could get by with four hours of sleep each night. I was getting about nine. Most important, the strength of *our* connection was growing step by step. That feeling was visceral.

17
"EL CAMPINO": LIFE IN THE ALBERGUES

At seventy-one, going back to a barracks-style existence didn't seem that appealing. Fortunately for me, Jacob was happy on the bunk above me so I generally got the bottom bunk, which was great until I'd sit up abruptly and hit my head on the wood above. With such high ceilings in virtually every dorm room, why was there was not enough headroom for the bottom bunk? I managed to forget this every night so at least once each evening I had an abrupt reminder and then again in the morning—slow learner. Regardless, from day one my bunk and I developed a solid rapport, whether the mattress was soft or firm. There was no time or option for the Goldilocks syndrome; you took what you were assigned and, believe me, they all felt good after you finished your daily twenty to thirty kilometres.

The thought of a short siesta after checking in still warms my heart, a distinct joy of the Spanish culture—*peregrino*-style. But there was a routine to follow. First, you had to check in. The accommodations were inexpensive: five to eight euros per bed at most locations, but you had to show your pilgrim's credentials to gain access. Equally important, once you reached Santiago, you had to show your credentials stamped each day to show your progress and qualify for your Compostela (the certificate you receive for walking the Camino). I have two, one in

Spanish and a second one in Latin. The former is only available if you complete the full eight hundred kilometres and cost me three euros. To get either you have to show your passport with stamps from every location. The Latin certificate is given to anyone who completes one hundred kilometres starting in Sarria or more. To me, this acknowledgement of a lesser achievement speaks to tourism. But are those recipients serious pilgrims? Their claim to having walked the Way diminishes the commitment of those who walk the entire route. To come remotely close to experiencing something like medieval pilgrims, it should be one continuous path beginning to end, but that's a personal opinion. The tourist or business aspect produces a wide range of options requiring equally variable effort and commitment. Jacob and I were all-in from Day 1 to Day 36.

A little more detail regarding our end-of-day routine. I sat down like a zombie (the last two kilometres of the day can make you feel like one), while Jacob used his improving Spanish skills to secure the bunks for the night. After leaving your shoes on a rack and walking sticks somewhere close to the main door, you limped to your designated room and experienced the unbridled joy of removing your backpack. Rest was in sight. But first you had to cover your mattress and pillow with the paper covers provided. I never quite perfected getting those flimsy covers on my mattress smoothly, but I became excellent at ripping them off in the morning when a little aggression in the face of yet another walk didn't hurt. Once your pack was off and your bed was covered, it was time for a shower or laundry or both. A lesson here worth repeating: take maybe two days' worth, or less, of clothes and do hand-laundry every day. You can lie around in your sleeping gear waiting for it to dry and we usually did. I very quickly got over any inhibitions of sharing dorms with the ladies. We were all just tired pilgrims seeking comfort from the road and none of us cared too much what we looked like.

Our experience with the albergues was totally positive. Travelling in the fall helped because there was never a problem getting a bunk, with several hostels to choose from most nights. I call them hostels because they pretty much fit the mould of what we think of as student travel stops. However, the word *hostal* in Spanish means a small, limited-service hotel, which is quite different than what we perceive hostels to be *and* more expensive. Great to stay in once or twice when you want a little privacy and you will. The true hostels or albergues themselves were clean, friendly, and welcoming. Every night brought a new connection or a number of reconnections as you shared stories of the day, discussed your blisters (somehow, neither Jacob nor I got even one), figured out where to eat that night, and most importantly jointly figured out how many kilometres to go to Santiago. Most of them had kitchen facilities, but more often than not we went out. Some offered dinner and breakfast prepared by the owners or by the volunteers, especially in the smaller villages.

That's when we enjoyed some intimate communal dinners and got to know fellow pilgrims better. While most nights followed the same pattern, every albergue was unique depending on the location within the community, the community itself, how they were funded, or who ran them. Some were *donativos* (by donation only) run by volunteers, some were run by the municipalities, some were private, but regardless, each one offered a similar but different experience. The evenings brought the security and comfort of *campino*: the same warm feeling you experienced as a kid if you went to summer camp. We even had a couple of singsongs orchestrated by volunteers. During the day we were often on our own, but at night we came together, all of us having faced the same challenge with different results. My good days weren't good for everyone nor were my bad ones universally bad, so the evenings brought a lot of encouragement when you needed it the most. Much like camp, we often shared the same meals, a bottle of wine, stories from home, different insights, and, when lucky, the opportunity to laugh at ourselves or the events of the day. After dinner I was usually back in my bunk by eight-thirty reading my guidebook about the next day and beyond. Earplugs went in at 9:59 and lights were out, with the exception of a few phones, promptly at 10:00.

18
THE LITTLE BLACK PILLOW

About a month before Jacob and I left for Spain, Karin and I went to Mountain Equipment Co-op (MEC), one of Canada's best known outdoor supply stores. We were looking for the essentials: the most suitable backpack and the best fit in footwear. That day I bought the wrong backpack. It fit well but was far too big, which is only a source of temptation to add more and a nuisance when you have to check your bag on the flight over. Jacob found that out the hard way when they lost his bag. Fortunately, I held off on the shoes and found the perfect pair a few weeks later—a great pair of Keen Koven hikers that fit my orthotics. (Worth repeating: Be diligent about your search for shoes or boots and definitely buy a size up.) Once I had my oversized pack, we looked around at all kinds of less "essentials," which were anything but. Don't try to anticipate every problem. As mentioned, take as little as possible and buy what you need when you need it. Your pack should be no more than forty-five litres, which is perfect for the carry-on requirement. If you accept that, your Camino just got easier. But you won't.

Anyway, shopping at MEC for the upcoming adventure was fun. While there we met John, who did buy his hiking shoes that day. After a short conversation he revealed that he was off to walk the Camino starting about two weeks ahead of Jacob and me. He seemed to be as committed as I was, but then he revealed that he didn't need a large pack because he was actually going on a tour, bussing the Camino, stressing that he would be walking short sections each day while his luggage was transported ahead to his pre-booked hotel room. The planned tour involved walking five kilometres each day before rejoining the bus. Nice! Moreover, he was seventy-one years old so he felt there was nothing wrong with doing it that way. You have to understand that John was just ever-so-slightly pompous. When he found out that I was doing the Camino as well, he asked me what tour I was going on. John was the first pseudo-pilgrim whom I met. In fact, that might be the day that the phrase was coined. When John found out that we were going on a self-guided hike (directions are no big deal when you understand how well the Camino is marked), he was mildly impressed. When Karin told him that my travelling companion was our grandson, who was intent on walking every single step, John became quite reflective, stopped talking to us, and soon left the store. I didn't have the heart to tell him that I was turning seventy-one as well. More than once as I was struggling up a steep hill in Spain, the thought of John far ahead sitting in an air-conditioned bus entered my slightly damaged psyche. No jealousy there; in fact, the reaction was surprising. Just the thought gave me the impetus to push on, motivated to make sure that every step was taken.

As we were standing in the checkout line, flanked by piles of small sale items meant to be impulse buys, Karin spotted a small black collapsible pillow in a drawstring bag. It was on sale for seven dollars and it weighed very little. My wife hadn't suggested much but that intrigued her. "You should take this. Who knows what kind of pillows you'll get in the hostels." I was skeptical, but for seven bucks I could trash it if it didn't work out so we bought it.

Well, that little black pillow was the one constant in my sleeping habits no matter where we were or how noisy the snoring was that night and no matter how hard the bed was. It fit perfectly under my chin and against my shoulder and it felt good: satiny and cool. It became my security blanket of sorts. If I lost it during the night, I scurried around the bed and on the floor until I found it, then right back to sleep. Silly, isn't it? But when you're in the midst of a physical challenge in unfamiliar circumstances, you latch on to things or people that you least expect.

You strike up conversations with unlikely fellow travellers and find common bonds where you were sure none existed. You ravish down food you would normally pass on eating. And those targeted eight glasses of water that you're supposed to drink every day but never quite do at home—well, they're downed by noon.

I'm ashamed to admit that I'm still using my little black pillow, even after being back from Spain for several years. It's pretty flat now but still has that cool satiny feel. The lesson, if there is one: find yourself some unlikely lightweight article that brings you comfort because you'll need it. Physical comfort is in short supply on the Camino.

19
MORNING MALAISE

Early morning is my least favourite time of day and that's an understatement. I lived in residence at university for the first three years and made it to exactly seven breakfasts, five of which were after all-night essay assignments. Note that the assignments weren't all-nighters, but my procrastination made them so. By the way, the first of the seven breakfasts was my first day. My residence nickname became Mono because I wasn't easy to wake up for a nine o'clock class.

At seventy-one, nothing had changed. But as in so many other areas, the Camino dictates timing. Lights were out at ten in the evening and came back on at seven in the morning. Pilgrims had to be out of the albergues by seven-thirty so the rooms could be cleaned and ready for new arrivals that afternoon. The "morning" people couldn't help themselves so there were muted activities as dark shapes glided around the room, flashlights in hand as early as five-thirty. This definitely happened in many of the smaller villages because in Spain the cock does indeed crow and he does it at five-thirty regardless of how dark it is. Packing and dressing in the dark just don't have much appeal for me. Walking in the dark has even less allure. Do bring a decent flashlight; that is a definite essential. Of course, your phone will suffice.

Having said that, you haven't lived until you experience the startling flash as the lights come on all at once at seven o'clock. One morning this was followed by a rousing rendition of some Italian folksong, belted out enthusiastically by six or seven jovial Italian guys travelling together. Ach, morning people! These were the same guys who after a few bottles of wine went to bed around eight-thirty at night, chatting incessantly so I couldn't read. And they snored even louder than they sang. As I woke up reluctantly, the song sounded vaguely familiar. After bumping my head on the bottom of the top bunk, I finally realized they were singing "She'll be coming round the mountain when she comes" in Italian. Unlike certain love songs that sound much better in Italian, this one simply doesn't cut it. Even more so when it reminds you that you have a steep seven-hundred-metre climb that morning to reach O'Cebriero. Just one example of albergue living. There is no choice but to conform: eat, walk, and sleep, pretty much on the same schedule as everyone else. Fortunately, the singing only happened once, but the image of the "choir" is etched in my memory as a typical Camino morning.

The irony here is that daylight in the fall season in Spain mimics my normal pattern, arriving around eight-thirty or even later—very civilized. This quirk happens because Spain remains on daylight saving time until the end of October and the country elects to be on the same time zone as continental Europe. However, if you check the map, Pamplona is more or less directly south of London, and by the time you've walked to Santiago you're more or less due south of Ireland. In other words, western Spain should be in the same time zone as the UK, which if it were, daylight in the fall would arrive around seven-thirty.

As this phenomenon became more apparent, Jacob and I began to take our time in the morning. No sense rushing out into the dark cold air when we could comfortably be out of the albergue by eight, grab a café con leche and a snack by eight-thirty, and be on the trail as the sun came up. That became our pattern. Walking the Camino in the summer is quite different. Sunrise is much earlier. The weather is much hotter. The trail is more crowded and getting accommodation is less predictable. One of my new Italian friends who had walked part of the Camino in the summer told me that the average high temperature had been forty degrees Celsius. In order to cope he had been getting up at three o'clock each morning and walking until eleven or so before quitting. Clearly there's still punishment and suffering in pilgrimage, if you so choose. I would have hated his routine and would have missed so much by walking in the dark, not to mention getting lost a few times. So, we suffered those early awakenings, forced to enjoy that morning coffee as others moved well ahead of us, at least for the day.

Despite my inclination to start slowly and this pattern of getting a late start, the mornings were the most productive part of the day. Generally, we would have two-thirds of each day's walk completed by noon. I think this is normal because facing a twenty-five-kilometre walk requires you to put your head down and make some serious progress. There are few things more discouraging on the Camino than the prospect of a long way to go after lunch. By the way, although the Camino is life-changing for many in different ways, I've reverted to being a nighthawk and sleeping in late. It does seem much easier to write about the Camino at midnight than to walk it at dawn.

DAILY LIFE ON THE CAMINO

20

THE LONGEST DAY: THE GOOD, THE BAD, AND THE UGLY

The trek from Los Arcos to Logroño on Day 8 was demanding and longer than most stages at twenty-eight kilometres. Thanks to John Brierley, we knew this so we attacked it early. The morning flew by, and after leaving at 6:45, we made great time. The early start allowed for a couple of café stops, which meant two extra chocolate croissants, plus two more glasses of freshly squeezed orange juice and two more cups of café con leche each. That became our pattern for the rest of our adventure. After losing that quick twenty pounds, I realized that I had to pump up my calorie intake. Those croissants gave me the short-term energy that I needed and my weight levelled off. Eat what you like, but it needs to be more than your norm. Your Camino demands it. Your body will thank you. Nutrition be damned! Damn the calories! Full speed ahead, or maybe half-speed?

We arrived in Viana around 11:30, which left only ten kilometres to go. The two of us were relaxed and confident, feeling totally adjusted to the demands of our trek. For the first time since Day 1, we took a long leisurely lunch, resting comfortably in an outside café in the Plaza de Los Fueros across the road from the Viana Iglesia de Santa Maria. That put us in touch with some lesser-known local history. Most of us have some awareness of the Borgia family as a corrupt influence on the Catholic Church. Wasn't one of them a pope when popes were far from the saints they promoted? To those more well-read, Cesare and Lucrezia Borgia were borderline evil, renowned plotters and manipulators, suspected of murders, immersed in the convoluted politics of Rome around 1500. What I didn't know was that the Borgia family were Spanish. I did some research when I got home. Cesare was the illegitimate son of Pope Alexander VI, formerly Rodrigo Borgia, born in Spain in a village near Valencia. I won't bore you with more history. You can always google the infamous Borgias.

The significance for us that day was that Cesare, who was both a cardinal and a military leader, was killed in a battle nearby and was interred in the church in Viana. There is so much history in this area of Spain. On the Camino, one walks in the shoes of some quite famous people. So, after our second glass of wine we took a quick peek into the church before leaving Viana around 2:00 p.m. We made one major mistake. We were quite cavalier about being able to find water along the Way that afternoon and we didn't refill our water bottles. Up until that point, it seemed that we found public fountains with potable water at villages every four or five kilometres. An old saying states that the word *assume* makes an *ass* of *u* and *me*. We made a terribly punishing assumption. We didn't know it, but we were facing ten gruelling kilometres with no place to find water. Where was Brierley's guidance when you needed it?

The afternoon was brutal as the temperature reached over thirty-five degrees Celsius. Even worse, there wasn't a leaf in sight or a speck of shade to be had. Those ten kilometres seemed more like twenty. To make matters worse, we ran out water in the first hour. Jacob handled it well. I did not. Of course, he gave me his standard mantra when we hit some obstacle. "Gramps, pain is just weakness leaving the body." I didn't realize I was that weak. Regardless, early on I lost the battle to the sun and was dying on the vine the last two hours, trying to somehow finish a day that had turned from ease into hardship. My afternoon nickname for the rest of the trip was confirmed that day. Morning Gramps could turn into afternoon Grumps. Not every day, but maybe a few more than I planned.

I was pretty well wiped long before we finally settled into our albergue in Logroño. The entry in my diary that evening was simple: "I am completely out of gas. I think 24 kms is my limit." That night I called Karin and we had the first extended conversation of the trip, over forty minutes. I needed a pep talk. Our conversation was the perfect pick-me-up. This six-week period was the longest separation of our married life and both of us were feeling it. My longest business trip had been two weeks, which only happened once.

The phone plan I had charged me ten dollars for any day of use, basically unlimited calls for the day at that price. Up until then I had used it sparingly but after that night we talked more often. We also started exchanging a series of poems about love, walking, and isolation. Some we found and some we wrote. All heartwarming but most too personal to share. A better, free option to connect by phone is to use WhatsApp. Of course, Jacob found that out during our trip and later made good use of it calling and texting his girlfriend in Australia.

I laid low that evening while Jacob went out for dinner with a group of young people from France, Algeria, the UK, the United States, Canada, and Korea. How neat is that and very typical of what your Camino experience will be. As for me, I picked up fruit and two quarts of juice from a *supermercado* close by and studied my faithful guidebook. I was soon dreading the thought of walking another thirty-plus kilometres the next day. This was one of the two or three stretches laid out that involved back-to-back walks totalling sixty kilometres or more. A lesson for you: always fill up your water bottle when you get the chance. The next fountain may be a long way off. By the time Jacob came back, I'd made an executive decision. We were breaking the next day into two easier ones: first going to Navarrete and then on to Nájera.

21
UN MÉDICO, UN MÉDICO

That proved to be a great decision. For the most part, those two days went well. On our way out of Logroño, we walked for more than an hour in a beautiful extended park, Parque de la Grajera. We stopped along the shore of the reservoir, swans and all, at a very nice café; one of the most relaxing breaks on the whole trip. Much needed for me after the stress of the previous day. Best of all, we were finished walking early, reaching Navarrete by 12:30. After a slight hesitation, we decided to indulge ourselves by renting a room in a hostal. As I've mentioned, that's a small hotel with amenities that seem luxurious after nights in a dormitory setting: no curfew, no lights out, no time limit in the (private!) shower, no snoring, plus great Wi-Fi for Jacob. Other than my almost flipping over the railing and falling three floors onto a hard tile floor, that first day was uneventful—except for the extra comfort. It was the only day until we reached our goal that we strayed from our dormitory existence and was well worth it. Besides, staying the course to being true pilgrims meant rejecting the temptation until we reached Santiago de Compostela.

Navarrete provided us a second brush with a history that I knew nothing about until recently. There are a number of different Caminos travelled in Spain. Most do end up in Santiago de Compostela, focused on the legendary resting place of James the apostle. A lesser-known path, perhaps more meaningful to members of the Catholic faith, is a brand-new modern pilgrimage known as the Ignatian Camino. St. Ignatius of Loyola was a soldier turned priest who founded the Society of Jesus, the Jesuit Order. Ignatius was his Latin name, but he was born in Loyola in the Basque region of northeastern Spain and given the Spanish name Inigo. This area lies just north of our route on the Camino. As Inigo, St. Ignatius was wounded in a battle near Pamplona. As he tried to find his calling, in 1522 Inigo walked from his home in Loyola to Monserrat and labelled himself "The Pilgrim." He was actually setting out for Jerusalem, but in Monserrat he stopped at the shrine of Our Lady of Monserrat in Catalonia. This is the basis for a new pilgrimage, anchored solidly in religion, from Loyola to Monserrat, a twenty-day journey that was initiated in 2023, five hundred years after Inigo began his journey and his conversion to St. Ignatius. Will it, too, become famous and well-travelled? These two routes happen to converge in Navarrete, where we spent the night. The Jesuit Order that he founded was devoted to the Pope, who sent them out as missionaries, acting as his "army" to boost the Counter Reformation. Among many other areas, they came to Canada shortly after their founding. Perhaps the best-known martyrs in Canadian history are Brothers Lalement and Brébeuf, Jesuit missionaries who were canonized in 1930 and are still celebrated by many who visit Sainte-Marie among the Hurons in Midland, Ontario. This was another brush with history as Jacob and I, like St. Ignatius, walked the streets of Navarrete.

The next day, moving on to Nájera started like a dream that soon transformed into a nightmare. The walk that day had been a breeze. At last, my pack and I were one. Twenty-eight pounds had become the new norm so we sailed into Nájera at noontime on October 1. As it turned out, that was an auspicious day; at least by the end, certainly a memorable one. As we walked through the town of about eighty-five hundred, a lot was going on. It was Saturday and the streets were busy with people in a festive mood. Never did find out why because we soon found a diversion of our own.

In the midst of all this activity, we settled down on a bench to choose an albergue for the night. We were right in the centre of town, along the banks of the Rio Najerilla. For some reason I stood up, slipped, and twisted an odd way, sending a shooting pain through my abdomen that caused an unintentional yelp. Unexpected pain can do that to you. An older Spanish gentleman heard me, undoubtedly noticing that I had grabbed my side at the same time. He spoke no English and was probably my age or younger, but as he rushed toward us, cane in hand, there was no mistaking the concern in his animated voice as he pointed to his left repeatedly and kept saying, "Un médico, un médico," which means "doctor" in Spanish. That much I knew; as well as the fact that the last thing I wanted to do was go to one in a foreign country. Surely, this was just muscular, maybe a cramp. The fact that we spoke little Spanish didn't deter our would-be benefactor.

While I tried to reassure him and Jacob that I was fine, he quickly called over two policemen who also spoke no English but joined in the chorus of "Un médico," offering to drive me to a clinic. At least that's what I thought they meant. I just wanted some breathing space and declined, handing my pack to Jacob and heading over the bridge to the albergue on the other side. Our concerned friend followed us all the way, continuing to call out "Un médico" while probably muttering "Loco" under his breath, still gesturing toward the apparent location of the doctor's office. Once we went inside the albergue, he disappeared but of course he was right—we just didn't know it yet. All I wanted was to lie down and let the pain subside. Jacob did his usual job of checking us in. Wisely, we took a rarely available double room, allowing us to skip the larger dormitory. I settled down to relax and get the pain under control while Jacob went out to buy some lunch. By the time he came back, I was writhing on the floor, dressed only in my underwear and a T-shirt.

And that's exactly how I exited the albergue in a flurry of confusion. Afterwards I found out that they couldn't get an ambulance quickly so we headed off in a taxi. I thought we were going to the hospital, but there is no hospital in Nájera so it was some type of clinic, with nurses and a doctor on site on a Saturday, certainly more than a private practice. No one spoke English so with a lot of gesturing Jacob and I tried to explain what was happening. Frankly, I wasn't sure if I had severe cramping or was in the midst of a heart attack. The biggest thing on my mind was *Oh no, our trip is over*.

Within a few minutes I had an intravenous feed in my arm and was lying on a stretcher awaiting an ambulance to take me back to Logroño. In the meantime, Jacob had phoned Karin in Canada, gotten the details of my prescription medication, and then disappeared. You can imagine how frantic I felt as they loaded me into the ambulance in his absence and the relief that followed when he came running back with both our backpacks and of course his sax, just before the driver pulled away.

This should not have been a time for humour. However, the IV was working and the pain was subsiding. Jacob pointed out that he had never been in an ambulance and to his surprise neither had I. That warranted a number of selfies showing the two of us in the ambulance, followed by a quick call to Karin, who was confused and concerned, and finally some serious discussion based on the likelihood that we wouldn't be able to continue. If he was afraid, he didn't show it. Jake stayed calm and took care of everything. I was pretty useless in the moment. But before we could resolve that issue, we arrived at the hospital and I was whisked into the emergency room while Jacob had to go to the admitting department.

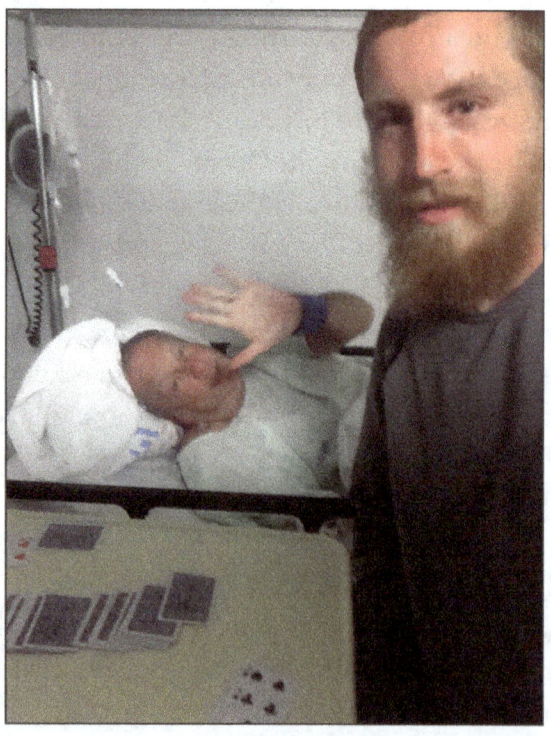

Certainly, the most discouraging thing was that the trip might be over, highlighted by the symbolism of going backwards speedily over a route that had taken hours to walk. Just going backwards was a mental setback. Our anxiety increased because we didn't see each other for almost three hours. In the meantime, I had X-rays and bloodwork and several animated conversations with my nurses and a doctor, none of whom spoke English. Finally, when I was exclaiming, "Donde es mi nieto?," which I hoped meant "Where is my grandson?," one nurse took pity on me and Jacob was allowed in. I was so glad to see him. In return he looked relieved. I can't imagine what he was thinking but he didn't hesitate to give me a very welcome big hug. His first words were "Don't worry, Gramps, whether the trip ends now or not, it's been great." But there was no way I was giving up that easy.

By that time, I was feeling fine and speculating that I could continue. We spent the next three hours playing cards and talking, with me assuring him regularly that I was positive I could resume. He wasn't so sure. We still don't know exactly what caused the problem; some combination of dehydration, constipation, strain from carrying my pack, who knows? Regardless, by nine o'clock I had been released with an admonition to reduce the weight I was carrying, a three-page report in Spanish confirming what had been done, and a very healthy appetite since I hadn't eaten much all day. At least I think that was what was said.

All I know is that I couldn't say *muchas gracias* enough to show the gratitude I felt. The experience was phenomenal. Despite the language limitations, the care I received from these warm, welcoming people was excellent and bolstered my confidence. Everyone was all smiles when we left as my nurses and my doctor wished me a "Buen Camino," clearly their encouragement to keep going. The language of caring is universal.

Jacob and I had lots to talk about, starting with the staff, my health assessment, and what we could do to lighten the load. Good mood or not, the taxi ride back to Nájera was much less fun than the ambulance ride. When we got back to the albergue, the owners, a husband-and-wife team, greeted us, showing a lot of concern. It's probably not a good sign for business if a *peregrino* dies in your albergue. Not knowing what to expect, they had held our room for us. They were very gracious, telling us to take our time leaving the next day or stay over if I needed the rest.

When we moved upstairs, I went to the washroom while Jacob headed to our room. When I came back a, nice-looking lady was talking to Jacob in the doorway and they were laughing. When she saw me, a torrent of Spanish came out of her and she grabbed my face, kissing me on both cheeks, and then planted a very firm kiss on my mouth. She was obviously very glad to see me, but I had no idea who she was. After she left, I asked Jacob, only to find out that she was the sister of the owner's wife, and she had checked us in earlier and also called the taxi to take us to the doctor. I'm pretty sure she didn't think she would see me alive again based on my condition when we left, so a nice surprise for both of us.

The next morning, we were up at seven and on our way to Santo Domingo, only twenty-one kilometres away, just another day on our Camino, our Way. Everyone's Camino *is* different, but very few have an experience like mine of that day. What was really important was that the countdown continued. There were only five hundred and eighty of those annoying yet fascinating kilometres left until we reached Santiago. That was the moment that I knew I had become a real pilgrim and that I would complete the pilgrimage. Officially, I always knew that I would, *but,* from that point on, I was sure.

22

THE GRAPES OF PATH

Fresh out of the hospital and given a second chance, I was soon offered a nice diversion. Logroño, Navarrete, Nájera, and the next town, Santo Domingo de la Calzada, were all in La Rioja, by far the smallest of the four provinces we walked through in Spain. It might be my personal favourite. To be sure, I have great and distinctive memories of all four, but La Rioja is special. Logroño is the capital city, located just over the border of Navarra. Although the hospital there is now my favourite in Spain, our first two days in the area had been challenging, to say the least. But the very best part of this distinctive province was in the open rural area: the vineyards. La Rioja has a flourishing wine industry. A common representation of the Camino in videos or photographs shows pilgrims walking beside or through row upon row of grapevines laden with abundant bunches of grapes. It's a very real and sublime experience but only lasts for those three days. We probably should apologize to the owners of some of these beautiful properties for our impertinence in doing repeated taste tests of their ever-so-attractive products. Actually not, for a good reason: to taste the grape of the country you visit, whether as wine or as fruit, is to understand that country better, so muchas gracias, Espana. In all probability, every peregrino gives in to temptation at least once along this part of the Way. In our defence, the weather was very hot for early October and the water we were carrying was always warm and tasteless, having just one redeeming grace: it was wet. But the grapes were so much better, like the nectar of the gods. At least they seemed that good to me when I was tired, hot, hungry, and thirsty.

Don't mean to sound like a travelogue but La Rioja is like a bridge: the transition between the steeper mountain walks of Navarra (where we entered Spain through the Pyrenees) and the flattest area of the Camino, the plains of the Meseta in Castilla y León. It's a nice compromise between the challenge of the mountains and the boredom of the plains. By far the most plentiful variety of grapes we encountered was a type of red grape that was more of a purple shade. We never did find the names of the various types, no time to research that. Those purple ones reminded me of the grapes my parents grew in our backyard that seldom made it into the house because my brothers and I would nibble on them incessantly throughout the summer months. Jacob and I polished of several bunches of these, which tasted so sweet and juicy, while sitting in the shade of the vines themselves because there seemed to be few trees around. It was the simplest of pleasures in a simple environment, definitely special to enjoy with your grandson. The temperature of the grapes didn't matter, they were so delicious. After a beautiful snack like that you are rejuvenated, good for the next two to three hours, until temptation strikes yet again.

More rare but even more juicy were the white or green shade of grapes. We saw a lot less of these along the Camino, which only made them more desirable and tastier to a hungry pilgrim. It's hard to describe just how laden the vines were, but even so we saw little evidence of harvesting. There were a surprising number of bunches just lying on the ground, which was a reddish clay colour. Maybe it was too early because we saw very few people as we walked along or through these properties, adding to the temptation. For sure, the sax solos sounded better with a full stomach and a wet throat. Even the sticky fingers didn't hamper the joy of some music while sitting on the ground surrounded by rows and rows of grapes soon to be wine. The natural sugar stoked up our energy levels, making the walks in La Rioja a little easier, even the uphill portions. Perhaps that's part of the psychological aspect of the

Camino process. First the pain and discouragement of the early mountain days, followed by a sense of accomplishment of getting through that phase and reaching Logroño, then a reward of sorts in the vineyards of La Rioja, which only lasts for three or four days and then you come upon the Meseta, which seems like it will never end but of course it does and then you find more mountains. At that point, you are battle-tested and you can appreciate the beauty of the mountains. All of it is memorable and part of a unique way to see a country.

Walking forces you to slow down and smell the roses and actually look at what there is to see. There is plenty of time to talk and observe and learn about the country and about each other. A much different experience than what you get on a whirlwind guided bus tour, which basically allows you to recite your visit to all the highlights of the country without achieving any sense of taste, smell, and touch that actually define a life quite different than your own. Friends have joked with me about the ABC tour of Europe: another bloody church, another bloody castle. It's all right to like churches and castles because they encapsulate a great deal of the history of Europe and I love history. There is plenty of opportunity to see both along the Camino, yet they are but a small part of the total Camino experience. I will always savour that thought and imagine the taste of the grapes of La Rioja, which appeared magically at the exact time when I desperately needed a boost.

23

THE HAUNTING SOUND OF THE SAXOPHONE IN THE MOST UNLIKELY OF PLACES

The next day we left La Rioja behind and moved on to Castilla y León, the largest province, where we would walk for the next sixteen days, almost half of the journey. This segment includes the cities of Burgos and León itself, stretching all the way to Galicia. First up was the small town of Belorado, about two thousand people, after a fairly straightforward walk of twenty-three kilometres. We were closing in on a third of the trip. This was the first time we stayed at an albergue that was donativo—by donation only. These welcoming shelters are usually run by a religious order and staffed by volunteers, almost always people who have completed their own Camino and want to give back. The concept of the donativo is that you donate what you can afford, the intent being to help people who have less to make their pilgrimage. The facilities can be quite minimalistic, as they were in Belorado. Maybe that's why we were slightly apprehensive about staying there, but the central location was close to the Church of Santa Maria and, very important, to restaurants. I am not a religious person so the latter was most on my mind when we stopped for the night.

The experience turned out much different than expected. The

facilities were small so no more than a dozen pilgrims were there that night. The hosts were volunteers from Switzerland. I've forgotten his name, but his wife was Ruth. After we returned from dinner, we were invited to join a few others while our two hosts offered us wine, cheese, and conversation. That's when I learned one of the more interesting facts about the Camino. Back in medieval times, it seems that many pilgrims were less willing than their present-day counterparts. Murderers and thieves were often sent on these pilgrimages on the premise that if they survived, they must be innocent and if not—well, that was justice. This was the reverse logic applied to suspected witches, women who were sometimes bound and thrown into the water. If they survived, they had to be witches because only witches could escape. Time to burn them at the stake. In the case of the reluctant pilgrims, apparently if God allowed you to reach Santiago, you must have had, quite literally, redeeming graces. That revelation shed some new light on a few of the founding pilgrims. Obviously, many pious people made the walk as well, with slightly less pressure.

As we talked, our hosts became increasingly enthralled with Jacob. Initially their interest stemmed from his young age and the fact that he was walking with his grandfather, a great icebreaker for us every night. Next was his name because Santiago is St. James (Santo Iacobi) and James is Jacob or Yaakov in Hebrew. We were walking the Way of St. James literally Jacob's way—very auspicious. Finally, they loved the fact that he was carrying his saxophone and encouraged him to play. At first, he was reluctant. They told a number of stories about various musicians and singers who had impromptu performances in the Church of Santa Maria right next door. Apparently, the acoustics in this fourteenth-century church were quite phenomenal, stemming from the time when much of the music came from the beautiful voices of the choir. Churches were designed to amplify the impact of those voices to the glory of God. All of this conversation served to increase Jacob's hesitation. Remember, he had only played the sax for one year in high school several years before and had purchased his current instrument just a month before. He was experimenting mostly with jazz, and one of his few complete tunes was Cole Porter's "Too Darn Hot." It was the perfect number as we walked the Camino on those scorching days but entirely too reminiscent of hell when inside a church. Fortunately for Jake, the church was locked up for the night so no worries.

No worries until the priest joined us for wine and cheese. He was in his mid-forties, a humble man yet one who was very proud of his parish and the historical role his church had played in the evolving story of the Camino. He spoke not a word of English but welcomed our broken Spanish, soon adding a torrent of words while speaking with our hosts. There was no way to say no to this gregarious fellow, who was soon calling me *abuelo* ("grandfather"), massaging my shoulders to help me relax, all the while coercing Jacob into a solo performance in his remarkable church.

Before we knew it his keys were out and we were having a private tour in extremely muted light, actually quite dark and a little eerie. Our group included Jacob and his sax plus me, the priest, our hosts, and one other pilgrim, a lady, who was strictly an observer. Unfortunately, I remember nothing about her. I had no idea what Jacob would do. As I sat there watching him at the front of the church, I had difficulty supressing a laugh at the idea of him blasting out "Too Darn Hot" in all the glory of the church. It didn't happen. My grandson showed great maturity. From somewhere deep in his psyche, he summoned up a partial tune; it wasn't a recognizable piece, neither classical nor mystical but somewhere in between: just the right notes. The acoustics did not let our new friend the priest down, echoing Jacob's song exquisitely throughout that seven-hundred-year-old edifice of history, where generations had worshipped. I am far from religious, as is Jacob, but the mood was reverent and will stay with us both forever.

In celebration, we were given a first-class tour of several gated vestibules locked away from the public, including a close look at the ornate altar that showcased a vibrant image of Santiago. It was a-special moment to share with my grandson. Few pilgrims get such a singular opportunity to immerse themselves in the local history as we did. Religious or not, we respected that history and the sanctity that had accrued in this church over such a long period of time. Our priest was a happy man so our goodbyes were a crescendo of smiles and good wishes, ending with the traditional "Buen Camino." And then it was curfew time: that surreal moment ended, leaving us slightly stunned but having gained a dramatic experience of Spain in general and the Camino in particular.

24
WALKING MATILDA

As mentioned earlier, a major part of the Camino for anyone is the people you meet, the experiences you share, and the conversations you have. While walking the Camino remains a predominantly European pursuit, people from many other countries have participated, increasing the international flavour over the years. Any description of my Camino would be incomplete without discussing the impact of some of these groups from different areas as we travelled on our own but also in concert. Jacob embraced the solidarity of the pilgrimage, taking great advantage of the opportunity to meet people from all over the world. It was a significant part of his growth experience and mine. With his love of the outdoors, he has a natural affinity with Australians, and we encountered quite a few along the Way.

Here's a little background on two countries that have pretty significant connections. Canadians and Australians have lot in common, being from large countries with relatively small populations and a somewhat contentious British heritage. Both of us have had a slightly disproportionate impact on the world partially because we are in the top ten countries in terms of natural resources. Australia has the deserts and the tropics. Canada has the tundra and the artic. Roughly ninety percent of Australians live within a hundred miles of the coast, while about the same percentage of Canadians live within a hundred miles of the U.S. border. As colonials, we have a proud history of supporting our British forefathers through battles like Passchendaele, Vimy Ridge, Dieppe, and Gallipoli. History suggests that in doing so we appear to have been more expendable than we should have been. That's a different issue. In addition, we both have rather good relationships with our American cousins, often impersonating them in films.

It was fortuitous that Jacob and I had met Teresa and Kathy from Sydney on the first morning of our Camino. As I described earlier, we all stayed at that lovely B&B, La Maison Ziberoa, with our delightful host Marie Josée, in Saint-Jean-Pied-de-Port before starting our journey. Marie Josée had completed her own Camino years before so she sent us off with encouragement after a wonderful breakfast. We left together that first day and literally wove in and out of one another's lives for the next six weeks. Along the way we developed a valued friendship, sharing some hardships, adventures, and most important a good number of laughs.

We moved along more or less at the same pace until my little hospital incident, but then we reconnected in Astorga more than two weeks later. In the interim, we often wondered where they were and how they were doing. It was heartwarming when they rushed up to us with apparent concern, having heard that I'd been in hospital but not knowing any more than that. Laughter all around as we recited the story, emphasizing the better elements of that episode: taking selfies in the ambulance and my enthusiastic greeting from the owner's sister when we returned to the albergue in Nájera. As a bonus, we got to celebrate Kathy's birthday that night. Celebrations on the Camino don't last too long partially because of the curfew but mainly because of the fatigue.

We met many other Aussies. Michael was a lawyer from Sydney who liked to get an early start in the morning and often walked with us at the beginning of the day before pulling ahead. Trevor and Fiona loved to have an afternoon drink at the end of their daily walk. I even postponed my afternoon siesta a couple of times to join the couple and discuss some of the finer things of life, like where they had eaten the night before or how far they were going to walk the next day. Life is simple on the Camino, as it should be.

One Australian young lady—*young* is a relative term because she was probably in her mid-forties—exemplified the spirit of the Camino as much as anyone we met. We never spoke along the way and I never did get her name, although I'm sure Teresa would know. She had the worst luck with blisters and throughout the trip her feet were almost always covered in bandages. I fully expected her to drop out or fall behind, but she never did. Sure enough, when we got to Santiago she arrived shortly after. When we saw her in the square in front of the cathedral, she was quite emotional, with tears flowing. When she saw us, we finally spoke and got big hugs as she told us that seeing the two of us together all along the route, grandfather and grandson, had been so great. I thought her perseverance had been terrific. We had been aware of each other almost the entire way, each quietly admiring the other for very different reasons.

One of my favourite comments from an Australian was made by Jesse, who referred to me as "gangster" or "gangsta" because I was walking the entire eight hundred kilometres at age seventy-one. I think this was supposed to be a compliment, but who knows? Anyway, I later found out that Jesse was not a typical driven Australian outdoors type. He was around twenty-five and carrying a very light backpack, I mean ultra-lite, maybe three or four pounds. I thought he was smart to be travelling light until I realized that he had a lot more with him but was shipping it ahead every day instead of carrying it. Shades of John, whom I'd met back in Canada at MEC. I do sometimes wonder how much John enjoyed his bus trip, but, undoubtedly, he did. Regardless, impressing Jesse wasn't that much of an achievement because he himself was hardly "gangsta."

And then there were the two redneck ladies. Every country has rednecks, I just hadn't met any from Australia. A few days after the Logroño hospital incident, I settled in for a little post-shower, pre-dinner siesta while Jacob went off to wander the outskirts of the village, taking his sax along to play in seclusion. Our room was in one of the smaller albergues so just six bunk beds, twelve people. At the time, these two ladies were also in the room. One had already gone to bed and would end up staying there until after we left the next morning. She hated the Camino. It turned out they had barely started, joining in at

Logroño. Both were in their sixties. The one already in bed was quite overweight and now had huge blisters, to the point that they had taken a taxi for part of that day rather than do the walk. Both women were survivors of heart attacks and appeared to be in questionable shape. What were they thinking? Anyway, her companion tried to reassure her, suggesting they take a bus to Burgos, where they would reach the Meseta, which was flat and much easier, but the heavier lady wasn't buying it. She was adamant that she had taken her last Camino step and I believe that she stuck to that. The two wanted to talk and I was the only one there to engage.

Remember, this was October 2016 so Donald Trump was the topic of many conversations as the American election approached. These two ladies made Archie Bunker look like a socialist liberal. Donald was sure to save the world. Barak Obama was a terrorist, bent on spreading Islam, and should be charged with treason and executed. If Hillary Clinton won, Australia should cease all co-operation with the United States, et cetera. They went on and on for a good half-hour as I sat there gaping in disbelief about what I was hearing. While I didn't see them again, I'm sure they were thrilled with the election results. As for me, it gave me great material for my many new Australian friends, who went out of their way to disavow the two ladies. As I said, every country has rednecks and based on some recent trends more than most of us realized.

25

REDEFINING DELICIOUS

We typically describe food as delicious if it is exceptionally good or if it brings back unique memories such as foods we enjoyed in childhood at special times. Delicious can also be used to describe non-food events that are delightful or very pleasing, enchanting or charming. On the Camino, I learned otherwise. Food no longer had to be exceptional to be delicious. It didn't have to be unique, memorable, or tempting. It didn't have to be caviar, tenderloin, or lobster. It just had to be food.

When you walk twenty-five kilometres or so every day for more than five weeks, everything you eat is heartwarming. No matter how many times the pilgrim menu offers a very basic roasted chicken, you will love it. No matter how watered down the table wine you are served may be, you will love it. You will find the salads outstanding even if they're similar to the ones you nibble at when you're at home but, without exception, you will always clear your plate. That dry bread that the Spanish put on the table with every meal no matter how incompatible it is with what is being served, just scrumptious. Best of all, you will eat as much as you want and still lose weight. Jacob and I ate much more than normal, stopping at cafés two or three times a day as well as breakfast and dinner, and I still lost twenty pounds. Jacob somehow maintained his weight, but he literally out-ate me by a factor of four to one.

Another concept I re-evaluated is comfort, suggesting luxury or coziness, relaxation or contentment. For many seniors, the idea of sleeping in bunk beds on a thin mattress with a transparent paper mattress cover is the antithesis of comfort. One is comfortable in familiar territory where there is a physical, secure element that makes you feel good. Bunk beds, on which you hit your head while surrounded by people of all ages and both sexes lounging around in their underwear, do not compute in terms of comfort. Wrong again! Believe me, at the end of that twenty-five-kilometre day, those dormitories feel like a spa, even after a shower where the water consumption is restricted and the temperature is tepid at best. And those bunks will surprise you. There are few better feelings than knowing your "walk of the day" is complete and that it's siesta time as you settle into your sleeping bag for just a little rest on that super-comfortable ever-so-thin mattress on those very bunk beds surrounded by your new Camino friends who are experiencing the same feelings of relief and accomplishment.

That is one of the core messages of the Camino. The realization that the many things you view as essential before you start are not. Life on the Camino is simple: you eat, you walk, and you sleep. Every day you have a clear-cut goal. There are few distractions. Every day you accomplish that goal. How neat is that? Stereotypical comforts are few, but the alternatives you do find feel oh-so-good. This has nothing to do with pilgrimage, religion, or spirituality. The Camino is a simple reality check, one that will cause you to question the meaning of many things and put them into a new perspective.

26
THE GAMES PEOPLE PLAY

Thirty-plus days (in our case, thirty-six) of walking requires diversion. For many, this takes the form of soul-searching, whether grounded in the religion of youth or the experiences of life. Almost every pilgrim is searching for answers to some inner dilemma. There is lots of time to think. For others, much time was passed by making acquaintances from around the world, sharing conversations and stories of life in a different country. The experiences of the day and the expectations for tomorrow provided a lot of dialogue and distraction as well.

At times like this, an active imagination can be a real asset. I was looking for some small thing to hold on to that would make my journey easier, just something to override the sheer magnitude of what I was attempting. Sometimes thinking is best replaced by role-playing. As a student of history, I found it intriguing that almost every village had a story to tell and had played some small role in the history of the area that long predated the founding of my country, Canada, barely one hundred and fifty years ago. The stone structures that were so dominant were enduring, as were the tales that each would tell, if they could only speak.

The many new style windmills prominent along parts of the Camino skyline were a modern reminder of Don Quixote, though I wonder what Cervantes would think of row upon row of these "hulking giants" as potential adversaries for his good-natured hero. I tried to imagine myself trekking across Spain like the man from La Mancha, but that didn't quite work. Jacob was not exactly Sancho Panza, though he was certainly protective of me. Besides, this potential army of illusory opponents looked more like elegant white knights on the horizon preparing to defend against the Moors than threatening challengers for an eccentric Spanish knight of questionable nobility. I had no interest in imaging myself as Cervantes's flawed hero. At least that's how my imagination perceived the windmills and the character.

Plenty of colourful local history related to the defeat of the Moors, from the legend of Roland in the first stages of the Camino to the fact that El Cid was born just outside of Burgos. Somehow that didn't catch my fancy either. Dreaming of dramatic battles centred on religious conflict was a little sensitive in the age of ISIS and seemed best left alone.

I had a number of other options to consider as inspiration: from the fall of the Knights Templar, who had been very prominent in the region, to the days of Ferdinand and Isabella, which started the rush to open up America. Spain is full of history. On segments of the Camino you walk over sections that were once Roman roads. For at least two days I imagined being a legionnaire marching with my comrades with trepidation at the thought of reaching *finis terrae*—the end of the world. Marching was the right idea, but plodding along like a legionnaire destined to die far from home didn't seem that romantic and it was tedious.

About one week in, I latched on to an idea that worked for me. To fully appreciate it you have to go to YouTube and look up "Scotland the Brave," pipes and drums; it has close to twenty million views. Listen to it and imagine yourself walking eight hundred kilometres with that echoing in your head. You're no longer a plodding legionnaire fighting under Pompey the great; you've now become a fierce member of a Scottish regiment, the Black Watch, the 42nd Royal Highland, who actually fought against Napoleon's troops, right in Galicia. If you love the pipes as I do, that music is motivating. After settling on the idea, each and every time I needed to dig deep to climb an unexpected hill or pick up the pace at the end of the day, I summoned that tune to play in my head. It is truly great marching music, and it got me through times when

I would have just liked to sit down or take a bus or do anything but walk when I had to walk. Sometimes I imagined we were chasing the French to run them out of Spain. Other times we were being chased toward the sea, which actually happened to the British in 1809.

Jacob used music as well, often tapping into that extensive compilation of songs on his phone. I can't list all the music we shared over the five weeks we walked together, but I know it covered a wide range from jazz to rap, with many genres in between. We didn't always listen together. When Jacob had his earphones in, he would tend to pick up the pace ever so slightly, immersed in his own thoughts while I would lag behind, sometimes quite a bit before he missed me. In that situation, it's better to lead than to follow. On more reason why I relied on the music of the mind and my imagination.

The Camino can be lonely when you're dragging your butt, watching your walking partner pull farther and farther ahead. Times like that were brief and he always noticed, then waited for me, which probably frustrated him a little. Yet he never complained. Those were the times when "Scotland the Brave" saved me. The uplifting swirl of the pipes and beat of the drums echoing in my head made me march harder, determined to bridge the gap. Music can lift us from the depths of despair, even when the music and the despair itself are imagined. That upbeat tune diverted me from my tired legs and sore feet and, as music is prone to do, lifted my spirits to finish the day. Future pilgrims: find your own fantasy, whatever that might be, and keep it to yourself as I did, but do find some form of pick-me-up that works because you will need one.

The times that we shared Jake's playlists were joyful. The fact that he knew and appreciated music from my own youth was a pleasant surprise. All grandparents should have the opportunity to spend the quality time that I had with Jacob. We tend to put the younger generations into boxes based on their differences from us, underestimating our common bonds. We question their values, their motivation, their ambition, and their knowledge, all because of an unavoidable generation gap that is magnified by society's ever-increasing rate of change.

27
THOSE BEAUTIFUL YELLOW ARROWS

The most pressing concern you may encounter, from Day 1 on, is finding your route. But thanks to a parish priest named Don Elías Valina Sampedro (a name you will quickly forget, as I did), the chance of going the wrong way is minimal. Even less so when you travel with a keen-eyed grandson. What you won't forget is the priest's now famous handiwork: the yellow arrows that appear on buildings, pavement, signposts, trees, and distance markers, always pointing you in the right direction.

Don Elías was a visionary, and his arrows have become a critical symbol of today's passage. It seems that he was consumed with recreating the ancient historical path of the medieval pilgrimage, spending years studying the history of the Way of St. James. The modern-day Camino started slowly, with just a few partaking in the first years. By the early 1980s, roughly a thousand *peregrinos* would travel the journey of pilgrimage each year without the benefit of a clear-cut pathway. Don Elías saw the potential to rejuvenate his beloved pilgrim experience if only the Way could be clearly defined. Rumour has it that around 1985 he drove his Citroën across the north of Spain with a trunk load of gaudy yellow paint, an unmistakable colour, delineating the path to be followed. He fully expected this would lead to what he termed "an invasion" of people wanting to have an unforgettable experience. He was right. That is exactly how things have evolved. Unfortunately, Don Elías passed away in 1989 before seeing his dream fully realized. Every step a pilgrim takes is a tribute to his foresight.

I can remember only one incident where we couldn't decide which way to go. Much of the time on the Camino you are walking off-road. The main exceptions are walking in, out of, or through one of the five significant cities along the Way, but occasionally you will have to walk alongside a rural roadway. On this particular day, Jacob and I came up to a road that we had to follow. There were walking paths along the side in both directions and no arrows to be found. As we approached the road, we saw a young Korean lady who was walking by herself, standing there trying to decide which way to go. Just as we arrived, she decided to take the path to the left. She spoke broken English and when we asked her why she was going in that direction, she shrugged her shoulders and continued on.

Fortunately for us, Jacob had to relieve himself, apparently a healthy number two, which required him to cross the road to find cover to do his business. I was happy to take a break. As he was returning, he could see one of the yellow arrows ahead pointing clearly to the right. Oh-oh. By this time, our new Korean friend was about a kilometre away, about to go around a bend. We yelled as loudly as we could to no avail as we watched her disappear around the corner. We never saw her again. Usually, people reappeared off and on. We looked for her that night and for the next few days but no luck. I have dreamed of her several times, even recently, often screaming at her to come back, but she never hears me. In my dreams, I am distraught and inconsolable that we lost her, sometimes waking up in a cold sweat. Haunting, not my favourite Camino memory.

28

THE CROSS OF SAINT JAMES AND THE SCALLOP SHELL

I'm not sure exactly why but the scallop shell is another enduring symbol of the Camino, evidently going back to medieval times. Apparently, the shells were used to guide the original pilgrims to the cathedral in Santiago. Shell patterns often appeared etched on buildings to identify significant structures along the journey.

It's suggested that these shells are tied to the legend of Saint James and his journey to Spain. I was never quite clear how he got there. Some versions tell that he arrived by sea and was washed ashore, where the shells guided his path. Others suggest that he was beheaded in Jerusalem and his remains were brought to Spain. Whatever, the undeniable attraction of the ancient pilgrimage was to visit the cathedral where his remains were reportedly interred. Another theory is that early pilgrims carried scallop shells to identify themselves as religious travellers. Today, the pattern of the shell is often embedded in the sidewalks of the cities along the Way to help you navigate through the urban areas. They are not as easily spotted as the yellow arrows, which are tolerated quite well in the villages and small towns but considered unsightly in the cities. Fortunately, in the cities many of the locals are happy to direct you if you ask. If you have ever ordered the delicious coquilles St. Jacques in a restaurant, you have literally enjoyed a small taste of the legend because that is what inspired the dish traditionally served on a scallop shell. I sometimes order it as a reminder of my Camino. Tasty!

Jacob was quite taken by the symbolism of the shell. His fascination is the basis for a diversion we made in Léon. The story of that can wait unit later. Many modern-day pilgrims will attach a scallop shell to their backpack. They are sold as souvenirs from Saint-Jean-Pied-de-Port to Santiago. You can buy an actual shell to pin on or a sew-on shell patch. Jacob has both. I opted for the shell itself. Today, these shells are decorated with the Cross of Saint James, which is a red cross shaped like a sword with a fleur-de-lis on the hilt and on both arms. The sword celebrates the martyrdom of Saint James, who in one version of the legend was reportedly beheaded by a sword at the order of King Herod. The colour red was chosen to represent the blood shed by the martyred apostle.

A red cross on a white background is commonly used by Christians. The Saint James version, incorporating the sword as the cross, definitely originated in the Middle Ages, most likely during the Crusades. Its use as a symbol goes back to the wars against the Moors conducted across Spain. The Knights Templar, who were French in origin but played a significant role in Spain during the thirteenth century, wore a more basic red cross on a white background. It's these ties with history that captured my interest in the cross. I'm sure that it was an important image rallying the early Spaniards in defence of their homeland and in protecting the holy relics in Santiago. These ties emphasize what an historically significant area northern Spain is.

As I've said before and will again, the Camino often finds you walking in the footsteps of many unknown heroes of different eras. That was of great interest to me. For others, more reverent, it was the religious past of the area. From the physical challenge to the search for spiritualism, there are many reasons to embrace the Camino. To each their own.

SYMBOLS OF THE CAMINO

29

THE EVE OF DESTRUCTION

We left Canada on September 21, 2016, and arrived back on November 1, exactly forty-two days. During that time, the American election, Donald Trump versus Hillary Clinton, was in full swing. While we caught various reports of the shifts in the polls and so on, we were far from consumed about the election. It just wasn't relevant to our daily routine. Jacob and I did have some interesting discussions about the pros and cons of the candidates while walking. Neither of us were enamoured with Mr. Trump. Our perception from afar was that a win by Trump could lead to a lot of problems.

One day in the middle of our saga, I was overtired and looking for a diversion. For whatever reason, a protest song from the 1960s written and recorded by Barry Maguire kept echoing through my mind: "The Eve of Destruction." As we walked, I began to blurt out my own new lyrics relevant to the election, which went more or less like what I've included below. Jacob soon joined in, helping with the lyrics and singing along in full voice. It might make it easier if you looked up Barry's version to hear the tune and help you to sing along.

> Donald Trump wants to get elected
> But Hillary believes that she will be selected

Donald hopes he will lead the nation
But his policies focus on discrimination

The human race could face elimination
Or even worse eternal damnation
Minorities face mass deportation
While we all watch in fascination

And you tell me
Over and over again, my friend
How you don't believe
We're on the Eve of Destruction

He'll bring new forms of corruption
The result could be mass destruction
She could be the first female leader
Or will the voters allow him to beat her

We're here in the heart of Spain
Not feeling any of this election pain
By the time we're back, it'll be over
A good time to be a Camino rover

And you tell me
Over and over again, my friend
How you don't believe
We're on the Eve of Destruction
No, you don't believe
We're on the Eve of Destruction

This is just a sampling of our lyrics and they definitely leave something to be desired. I have left out some of the more colourful ones based on the *Access Hollywood* tapes and other developments at the time, such as the debates. But in the midst of a long day, with no one else around, Jacob and I found them hilarious. Another example of Camino crazy. We were soon bellowing out our modified protest song at the top of our lungs, laughing as we walked. Our off-key version echoed around the hills that surrounded us so we kept on singing, adding the occasional verse as we walked.

This particular distraction lasted more than two hours before a couple caught up to us. They were quite enthralled with our full-throated rendition and some of our lyrics. We walked together for a short while, during which the lady asked us to start from the beginning so she could video us. As we left them behind, while they took a break, she promised to put us up on YouTube (I don't think that ever happened). Regardless, another day passed quickly and we met our goal for the day, entertaining ourselves in the process and deepening the bond between us. The protest song from my youth translated quite well to the life and times of my grandson.

30
SEASONS IN THE SUN

An important decision to be made before you launch your Camino is when to do it. The pitfalls are significant. The weather in this part of Spain can be unpredictable. Winter is out for most of us, just too difficult for unseasoned trekkers. Early spring can be cool and wet. But spring is a beautiful time of year as the Camino reawakens after a quiet winter. While the numbers on the road will be much less than later, not all the albergues will be open so planning your days may be more difficult. Peace and tranquility are more certain, paid for by slightly less convenience. May and June can be good months weatherwise, warmer and drier, but the number of international visitors will be on the rise, offset by some degree by most albergues being open.

Most important: Avoid the summer if you can because that's when the intensity of the sun and the density of the crowds detract from your Camino experience. More than half of those walking in any particular year do so in July and August. While the daylight hours are longer, you may find yourself getting up early to walk in the dark, reducing your sun exposure, avoiding the hottest parts of the day, and arriving early at your target destination to ensure accommodation. That's how some of my Camino friends, repeat walkers, described their experience walking in the summer months.

More critical than that, I believe that the intimacy of the Camino, such an integral part of my personal experience, is diminished by the crowds. Familiar faces will be lost in the hordes of rotating new arrivals as the Europeans break their version of the Way into several years, one or two weeks at a time. Heresy for me to say, but in the summer the Camino pays a price for its success. Whatever season you choose, you must wear sun protection. The sun in northern Spain is intense.

Jacob and I lucked out. Walking in the autumn was the only choice we had. Jake was working hard under his tree-planting contract and I was busy trying to walk various distances to improve my stamina, looking for the right shoes and socks, and experimenting with the size of pack I would take. I didn't start any of these things until July because as much as I wanted this shared experience, I was sure that Jacob would change his mind, encumbered by the challenges and opportunities of the activities of a twenty-two-year-old.

The July 1 holiday weekend was a wakeup call. I realized that he was not going to cancel and worse, I was woefully ill-prepared to take on an eight-hundred-kilometre trek that I had to complete. If we went, I had to finish! No choice about it. Besides, if he was going, I had to go! There is no disappointing your grandson. As I mentioned, I have three other grandsons and two granddaughters so I'm trying to live up to the precedent I set with Jacob. Had it not been for COVID, I might have been able to try the Portuguese Camino with the next oldest, Gareth. However, more Caminos are out so finding a way to get that shareable experience is a promise I must find a way to keep.

Jacob and I set off literally on the first day of autumn, September 22, 2016, yet that first week felt like an extended summer, with temperatures in the mid-thirties Celsius. The rest of the weather was variable but never unpleasant. The number of travellers was small. Very few European holidayers joined us. For the first seven hundred kilometres, we enjoyed plenty of serenity. Lots of days we walked on our own for extended periods, meeting others at the cafés during the day or for dinner at night. It seemed a near-perfect blend, with enough people to make connections but no sense or impact of larger crowds. Almost all the albergues were still open so accommodation was readily available and extended walks to find a bed never happened. Thumbs up from me for the fall season.

The last hundred kilometres were not quite the same, but that's a tale for later.

31
THE RAIN IN SPAIN

Another vision that occurred to me when I had too much time to think while walking was that of Rex Harrison, as Professor Henry Higgins, cavorting with Colonel Pickering (actor Wilfrid Hyde-White) and Liza Doolittle (played by my favourite actress, Audrey Hepburn) as they recited (because Rex couldn't really sing), "The rain in Spain stays mainly on the plain." Clever little tune that sticks in your head under the right or wrong circumstances. But where was that plain? What part of Spain? Maybe the Meseta? These are the questions that boggle your mind when you're dragging a bit and your brain in Spain is suffering from drain that you can't explain. Brain-drain in Spain can happen on the Camino when you play silly mind games to ease the pain your muscles obtain. But enough of such temporary rhyming madness.

Jacob and I were forewarned that the fall could be quite wet. It was possible that we would have rain many of the days that travelled. We prepared for it, but excessive rainfall just didn't happen. Day 21 was the first day we encountered any rain whatsoever and we were five hundred kilometres in, with three hundred to go. My biggest decision of the day was when to take off my rain jacket. Would I rather be hot and sweaty or cold and wet? Usually, the coat came off. That day, we woke up to a fine rain on a misty day that lasted until about 1:30 p.m., followed by roughly an hour of sunshine and finishing the day with a cold and rainy stretch. That was by far the exception and definitely not the rule we had been led to believe.

The next day we had a brief light rain the last hour as we walked into Léon. No more rain until Days 31 and 32, with almost seven hundred kilometres under our belt. Overall, we had rain on about four days out of thirty-six, and never had an all-day heavy rain where we got drenched. I have to say: Henry Higgins, to paraphrase Shakespeare, that was all very much ado about nothing.

32
"WHEREVER YOU GO, THERE YOU ARE"
—CONFUCIUS

For those six weeks in the fall of 2016, walking was my life while talking with Jacob was my lifeblood. The essence of my trip was to build a lifelong bond with my grandson, but walking was such a major part of the effort. It's no surprise that I turned to researching meaningful thoughts and quotes about walking. Maybe I was looking for inspiration or maybe just the motivation to keep moving, but the longer we walked, the more relevant these became so here are a few to consider:

"An early morning walk is a blessing for the whole day."
—Henry David Thoreau

"Walking is the great adventure, the first meditation, a practice of heartiness and soul primary to humankind. Walking is the exact balance between spirit and humility."
—Gary Snyder

"In every walk with nature, one receives far more than he seeks."
—John Muir

"The journey of a thousand miles begins with a single step."
—Lao Tzu

"If you are in a bad mood, go for a walk. If you are still in a bad mood, go for another."
—Socrates

"Walking is man's best medicine."
—Hippocrates

"All truly great thoughts are conceived while walking."
—Friedrich Nietzsche

"Now shall I walk or should I ride? 'Ride', Pleasure said. "Walk', Joy replied."
—W.H. Davies

"After a day's walk, everything has twice its usual value."
—George Macauley Trevelyan

"As you start to walk out on the way, the way appears."
—Rumi

"If you have found a path worth to walk, never complain about walking!"
—Mehmet Murat İldan

"Paths are made by walking."
—Franz Kafka

"I felt while I was walking, a heart so full that life could have left me then."
—Albert Camus

> "Wandering re-establishes the original harmony that between man and the universe."
>
> —Anatole France

> "You have brains in your head. You have feet in your shoes. You can steer yourself, any direction you choose."
>
> —Dr. Suess

> "Golf is a good walk spoiled."
>
> —Mark Twain

> "I felt my lungs inflate with the onrush of scenery—air, mountains, trees, people. I thought, 'This is what it is to be happy.'"
>
> —Sylvia Plath

Add in the old stone buildings and that encapsulates my Camino experience.

There are many more such statements, all thoughtful, most requiring further scrutiny. It seems that humankind has reflected on the rewards of walking for time immemorial. I suppose such thoughts are the basis of pilgrimage, removing yourself from a mundane life to meditate, contemplate, postulate, gravitate, and speculate. All of these thoughts, some very old, some not so old, were relevant to me as I walked those eight hundred kilometres. At times, it seemed that all of these thinkers, many famous in their time, were walking with me on my Camino. Their thoughts were my thoughts, often expressed more vividly but relatable. I don't apologize for my vivid imagination. In combination, these various reflections seemed to define the myriads of feelings I was experiencing. My emotions were jumbled for those eight weeks and for some time thereafter. Life was so very different. Understanding why has been a challenge.

One last quote to consider:

> "There is no grandfather who does not adore his grandson."
>
> —Victor Hugo

That is why I walked my Camino. I knew this before we started. I revel in it since we finished. I have six grandchildren and that deep abundant love is the one sure thing I have to offer them all.

33
RECOVERY AND A CONFESSION

I really haven't described the aftermath of my hospital stay beyond saying that the next morning we were up and off as if it hadn't happened. Much of what I've been describing took place after that nonevent so it's evident that I continued, but how could I? The real trauma was not the actual health issue, which vanished soon after they put me on intravenous at the first clinic. The logical explanation is that I was dehydrated, but we didn't know that for sure. The language barrier at the hospital only added to the uncertainty. The overriding fear was that our Camino, long anticipated and off to a great start, was over. Could we continue on or not?

Ironically, with my weight loss, I was feeling great physically, but the attack (or whatever it was) had come on so suddenly it had left a threat hanging over our heads for the next few days. Jacob was a little overly protective of me, but I was basically fine. Before the event, we had often separated briefly at times as he pulled ahead or we each got into our own conversations with fellow pilgrims, but most of the time we were together. For that first week after our unexpected backwards visit to Logroño, we were inseparable.

After a few days we found another factor that could facilitate the rest of the journey—one that I hesitated to take advantage of at first. I suppose I was embarrassed to use a service that I felt would diminish my efforts to be a full-fledged pilgrim. I didn't want to become a pseudo-*peregrino* in any way. The macho element of my psyche resisted the very thought of taking any easier approach. Ultimately, I decided it was a better option than jeopardizing the chance for Jacob and me to complete our Camino.

I'm only admitting this because it might impact your judgment on whether you follow in my steps and take on your own Camino or not. You should, and this anecdote might give you some comfort to come walk with me, provided you take this book along. There is a service that will transfer your bag forward for you to whatever albergue that you designate. Back in 2016, that cost about three euros per day. All that it requires is a tag that you purchase, fill out, and attach. The bags had to be out early. I had noticed piles of bags out in the mornings but hadn't paid much attention to them. I soon found out that quite a few people were taking this option. While many were ladies travelling on their own, quite a few men were doing it, a few significantly younger than I was. Fortunately, I had a large black bag with me that I had put my backpack into for transit on the flight over. From that point on, I carried a lighter backpack with just the daily essentials and things I couldn't lose, like my medication and, of course, my copy of Brierley and my diary. The weight on my pack went down and so did Jacob's. Everything else that could fit went into the big black bag, our sleeping bags, extra clothes, whatever, but *not* the saxophone. As a result, I was carrying just under ten pounds.

This change in procedure added a little anxiety to the day. First you had to plan more carefully and commit with certainty how far you would go. Overtired or not, your goal was rigid. You had to catch up to your bag. No chance to stop a little earlier at a convenient albergue. Then you had that little bit of doubt each day—would your bag be there? After all, there was a mound of bags going out in the morning to several different destinations. What if they left your bag at the wrong place? What if your tag came off? It never happened. The service is very reliable. If this will make a difference, use it, and plan a Camino that will work for you. However, I do suggest that you forego the hospital visit.

34
CITIES OF THE CAMINO

There are five significant cities on the Camino Frances: Pamplona, Logroño, Burgos, Léon, and Santiago de Compostela. All are interesting. If you were on a conventional bus tour, you would spend hours walking their streets, visiting historical sights, especially their cathedrals, and enjoying their restaurants. When possible, you would experience a few of the many festivals that seem to pop up everywhere in Spain. That was not our context. As I prelude to my reaction when I got home, I could not get out of the bustling cities fast enough. My least favourite parts of our trek were the walks along busy roadways in and out of these typical fast-paced urban areas. I found them more of a diversion from the pleasant days spent in pastoral settings, walking through peaceful small villages with their old stone buildings and relaxing cafés that we'd experienced most of the time.

We hit Burgos after walking approximately three hundred kilometres. It was the first city that we took the time to explore, if only for a few hours. Pamplona was the first of the five that we visited and we were there twice, once by train and once on foot. Most of you know the name because of the videos you've seen of the running of the bulls, which takes place in July attended by huge crowds. Unfortunately, we didn't see much of Pamplona. The first time, we literally ran from the train station to the bus station to make sure we caught our bus to Saint-Jean-Pied-de-Port. The second time, when walking back (Day 4) we arrived in the midst of some kind of festival and streets filled with exuberant locals. Tempting but anxiety prevailed. We had to take a cab out to the airport to retrieve Jacob's backpack. We were totally focused on the airport, unsure if the bag had arrived. *If we didn't get it there, we weren't going to get it.* Regardless we saw little of the city itself. Of course, the bag was there waiting, but seeing much of Pamplona was not to be. Next time?

The subsequent city we encountered was Logroño, which we hit after the longest, most demanding afternoon of the entire trip (Day 8). We arrived after five in the afternoon, too tired to do any touring. The redeeming grace of that city was our walk out of it the next morning. A sound sleep, the night before, and the peaceful scenery certainly helped. This was an unrushed day. By breaking the proposed stage in two, there were only thirteen kilometres ahead. We exited the city through a grand park that extended beyond the city limits. As mentioned, at the end of the park we found a delightful café with a large patio overlooking a small lake, where we sat near a flock or bevy of swans and enjoyed a delicious ice-cream bar, taking our time. After the heat of the previous day, it was a welcome treat. A tough entrance and a pleasant exit. That's my memory of Logroño.

Back to Burgos (Day 14), with four hundred and ninety kilometres to go. The weather on the walk in was much cooler, much colder in the morning than previous days. The old city centre of Burgos is beautiful, highlighted by the majestic cathedral. Designated as a World Heritage site, the *Catedral de Santa María* dates back to the thirteenth century and is considered one of the most beautiful of the many in Spain. The inside features a wealth of art and artifacts. Other than in Santiago, this is the first city where we took the opportunity to be tourists. I suppose one could, maybe should, allow for at least an extra day in each city to tour but we had just two hours to view a cathedral that warrants so much more attention. This is not a huge city—less than 200,000 population. Pamplona was about the same, Logroño was closer to 150,000. Yet all have such a long interesting history, going back to medieval times and beyond. If these walls could only talk. What a contrast with North

America, where indigenous history is supressed and recent history is so short-lived. As much as I love history and I do, and as much as the Camino stimulated my imagination of past times, it was not the time for seriously exploring the past. It was much more an exercise of living in the past.

León and Santiago de Compostela have their own stories and our own experiences. Those will come soon. Burgos is where we said goodbye to the two MBA students—one Parisian (Eva), whose parents lived in Dubai; and one from Algiers (Sarah)—who had been part of our walk for the previous eight days. They were returning to school. Their two-week stint on the Camino ended there. I wonder if they went back to complete it?

This is also the last place we saw Fred and Marie from Salt Lake City, plus Antonio and Basia from Italy, as they all rushed to catch the train to León. I felt betrayed. We had spoken to Fred and Marie often and seen both couples many times over the previous two weeks. Fred and his wife were in their sixties, but the other two were in their twenties. Basia had suffered with blisters, but it never occurred to me that any of our compatriots would short-circuit things by jumping on a train. As they were entering the train station, Marie shouted back, "Enjoy the Meseta, we'll see you in Santiago." We never saw them again. Such is the Way—unpredictable and everchanging.

35
DEFINING FLAT

The first time I flew into Winnipeg as I walked on to the tarmac, I realized what flat terrain meant. It was like the song "On a clear day, (You can see forever)" or so it seemed. The area is described as "extremely flat topography." To this point in Spain, we had only experienced mountains and valleys, that is, until we hit the northern edge of the Meseta as we exited Burgos. That's the large flat plain located in the centre of the Way, in between the cities of Burgos and Léon: a stretch of the Camino that some people avoid completely. That's why several other people within our diverse free-flowing group also took the train from Burgos to Léon, skipping almost a quarter of the Camino. One more type of pseudo-pilgrim we encountered. Trains didn't exist in mediaeval times.

As for Jacob and me, the Meseta provided new opportunity. Boredom begets banter. We were having daily in-depth conversations covering new and numerous topics, including entrepreneurship, his upcoming trip to Australia, vertical farming, meditation, and the difference between "bold and brave" and "reckless and stupid," to name a few. He was interested and interesting. We'd never had as much time to talk about things in such detail before. I had been worried about Jacob's lack of interest in formal education. I mistakenly misread this as a lack of interest in learning. Walking together, I realized that much of the time he was spending on his phone was researching things that interested him. My own belief is that university is a tool—the bridge between teacher-led learning and ongoing self-learning for the rest of your life. To my great relief, I saw first-hand that Jacob has the ability and the interest to research and analyze independently. What I wished for him then and still do is to find happiness, whatever form that will take, but I now knew he would pursue opportunity in spades.

The talks were great. The landscape was boring. The Spanish *la mesa* means "table" so *meseta* translates as "plateau" or "tableland." To those who walk the Camino, it means more like "flat and boring," or worse: "long and drawn-out." My words because the area is indeed flat, very flat, and the distance is roughly two hundred kilometres. It does not appear at a good time in the midst of a long trek. Halfway there is the nice way of saying that you've got a hell of a long way left.

The next few days were when I relied most on "Scotland the Brave" in the playlist of my mind. Those days dragged and at times the end of the day seemed beyond reach. This was purely mental, as the Meseta was less challenging physically. I particularly remember one day when we were walking with Alex from Bulgaria, who was on his own. The last two miles we were literally marching briskly, three across. In my mind, the pipes and drums of "Scotland the Brave" helped me keep pace with my younger stalwarts. Lots of villages and cafés filled the days, but there was much less variety in the terrain. That helped somewhat.

We did have some excellent meals, but one stood out. It took place in a small village with a single albergue accommodating fifteen or so pilgrims. The host and hostess prepared the dinner, which was included in our stay. We were seated in a communal dinner setting around a large table. After a sumptuous salad, they brought out the most delicious chicken paella made with excellent rice, different than what I had before, mixed with fresh peas, tomatoes, and peppers. I had only had seafood paella before and thought the chicken one would suffer in comparison. Absolutely wrong. The conversation was flowing along with the wine and seconds were served. A memorable meal in the midst of less memorable geography. These onsite communal dinners were my favourite because the hosts took a personal interest in us. The meals were homecooked and were an improvement on those inexpensive *peregrino* specials served in restaurants.

It took almost eight days to traverse the Meseta. The notes in my diary are the most brief of the trip and focus mainly on the distances travelled each day and the food at night. Sleep, eat, walk—the same routine as before, the walks were just less stimulating. Even so, I would never take the train in order to miss what happened along the Way in those eight days.

36
THE TATOO OF LÉON

We reached León on Day 22, two days behind Brierley's thirty-three-day schedule. We had finally reached the end of the Meseta and we'd only seen the northern part. The entire Meseta extends southward well beyond Madrid and covers roughly two hundred and ten thousand square kilometres. We were not sorry to see it end.

León is a city of about 130,000. Putting things in perspective, Jacob and I lived in Guelph, Ontario, a city of 140,000, which is small by North American standards. We had now seen four of the five cities on the Camino and none of them were substantially larger than our hometown. They seemed larger. All of them were definitely much older, say a thousand years or more. All of them had massive cathedrals and so much history. León was the smallest and the oldest, originating as a Roman military post. I mentioned imagining the Roman Legions marching across Spain led by the Roman General Pompey, who, after his victories in Hispania, formed the first triumvirate with Julius Caesar and Crassus.

What a country as a setting for a history buff! This is why walking through a country is so different than taking a tour bus. Settings like this are a blip on the bus tour and are tough to remember when you revisit your extensive photo collection next year. But if you actually walk the entire area, they are indelibly logged into your memory bank. The annoying complaint of the ABC tour of Europe repeated by many bus tourists (another bloody castle, another bloody church) served up by a guide doesn't resonate the same when you walk/march/strut into town like a conquering hero on your own—just like one who did five hundred years or even a thousand years before. It's a very different experience.

The name Léon derives from the Roman word *Legion*, reflecting its early history. The walk into Léon was a relatively short eighteen kilometres so we arrived earlier than normal, giving us time to explore the city and, yes, there is a cathedral (*Santa Maria de Léon Catedral*) and a basilica (*Real Basilica de San Isidoro*). There is also a distinct medieval quarter. There was actually a Kingdom of Léon dating back over a thousand years. Enough recitation of history. We had a nice late lunch and an hour or two of walking the city after checking in to our albergue. I didn't feel like eating out so I went to a nearby *supermercado*. After picking up a chocolate milk, some potato chips, and bananas, I flaked out for the night and gave Karin a call. My countdown continued: three hundred and ten kilometres and thirteen days to go. We had completed sixty percent.

Jacob had reconnected with our English friend Tom and they went out for dinner together. Of all the people we connected with, Tom kept coming back into our life the most. He had just completed his PhD in economics. He was a bright fellow and I was pleased that he and Jacob got on so well. That night I had a very sound sleep and vaguely remember Jacob coming in and telling me that he wanted to stay over in Léon for an extra day because he had made an appointment. Staying over an extra day had been discussed earlier and rejected. I was half asleep and didn't pay much attention.

The next morning, he informed me that he had an appointment to get a tattoo at 5:00 p.m. I wasn't exactly pleased, but I bit my tongue. We had a leisurely day doing little other than booking into a much nicer albergue for our second night. We kept the appointment and I was shown the design of the tattoo, which was a medium-sized scallop shell, the symbol of the Camino, which was to be done just above the ankle. It was actually based on a picture Jacob had taken. The location was quite discreet and when asked, I approved. That invoked an offer for me to get one as well but that was politely declined. The tattoo parlour was clean and tidy and the owner was a nice fellow but I wasn't comfortable with the idea. A small generational divide, but I accepted Jake's decision without rancour and sat calmly by while the artist did his thing.

In retrospect, I kind of regret not getting my own, which would have accentuated our shared adventure with undeniable physical evidence. Matching tattoos would have added another dimension to the legend of the grandfather-and-grandson walking duo. For the next five days Jake looked after it religiously, wrapping it tightly and keeping it clean exactly as instructed. So, my most memorable moment in León did not involve a cathedral but rather a little shop around the corner that did quite artistic tattoos. Who would have thought?

37
THE GOOD SAMARITANS

One might think that the imposition of hundreds of thousands of strangers parading through many small communities would breed resentment among some element of the local population. If it did, we didn't witness the slightest sign of it. I suppose the counter-argument is that this unique form of tourism infuses life into the local economies, creating opportunity.

One of the most haunting feelings I had along the Way was when we walked through a village made up entirely of attractive old stone buildings without seeing a single person. It was like walking into one of the ghost towns from the American Wild West. While that was abnormal, it gave a sense that these, often ancient, communities are struggling. To be sure, there were signs of agriculture everywhere, with animals a welcome site, sometimes right in town, but most farms seemed small with questionable viability. Of course, there were exceptions to this, such as the large, healthy vineyards in La Rioja or the mammoth haystacks Jacob climbed or the huge fields of sunflowers we had seen ready to harvest the seeds. But the overriding sense was that business was not great.

El Camino was meant to be a transfusion of opportunity into these communities—a lifeline. That said, the reality is that villages offer much needed cafés, perhaps an albergue and a small restaurant, but little else.

None of these opened up significant employment opportunities. Travellers tend to gravitate to the larger towns, which offer more options for their overnight needs. Besides, pilgrims are not affluent tourists spending freely on expensive meals and guided tourists. The feeling of that empty village impacted me, leaving me with a sense of sadness. I thought back to the *salade, no atun* day and that small restaurant in one of the smallest villages with a single albergue. The restaurant could only hold about twelve patrons. It was run by the hardworking couple who served breakfast in the morning, lunch later, and were still serving dinner at 9:00 p.m. The owner was so frustrated by our overdone laughing and our inability to speak Spanish. The scene was hilarious but, given this different context of their challenging life, it doesn't seem nearly as funny. I feel a sense of guilt now but only after the smile crosses my face.

In contrast to this less inspiring vibe, the people of Spain seem a happy lot. Festivals were evident in the cities and towns every weekend. Kindness to pilgrims was evident everywhere. Badly spoken Spanish was welcomed with a smile. Jacob's persistent attempts to speak the language were always greeted warmly. The fact that we were *Nieto* and *Abuelo*, Grandson and Grandfather, travelling together always elicited positive reactions. The best words to describe how we were treated are: kindness, caring, thoughtfulness, and consideration. Maybe those reactions stemmed from the effort that we pilgrims were making. El Camino can be tough sledding.

One lesson from the parable of the Good Samaritan is that when you see someone under duress or in pain, you help them whether they're a stranger or even an enemy. That premise makes me think of a number of incidents. One time early on, Jacob and I arrived later at a small albergue. While he was paying for our beds, I sat down, undoubtedly showing my exhaustion. This very kind Spanish lady, the receptionist, noticed and took Jacob aside to show him something. When he came back, she had given us a private room with two beds. No extra charge. I hadn't gotten used to dormitory life yet so that act of kindness was a blessing.

Of course, there was the old gentleman who immediately noticed my discomfort the day I ended up in the hospital and suggested *un médico*, pointing the way and calling over the police to assist me. My hurried exit and my hasty *muchas gracias* hardly seemed enough. The ten or more people at the hospital who gave me several tests before sending me on my way with confidence. A number of people in the cities who when we couldn't find our way enthusiastically gave us directions, sometimes walking a block or two with us to make sure we were on route. These are but a few examples but always, and I do mean always, every act of kindness from the simple morning greeting of "Buen dia'" on was highlighted as you left by the traditional wish of the Way: "Buen Camino"—Happy Trails.

38
A TYPICAL COMMUNAL DINNER

The day after leaving Léon, we extended our day a little because the following day would have been more than thirty kilometres. Our countdown went below three hundred kilometres as we walked. We arrived at San Martin a little later than usual and managed to find an excellent albergue that served both dinner and breakfast, apparently including some excellent desserts.

At the dinner that night, we had quite an assortment of pilgrims forming a significant international assembly, none of whom we'd seen before. Maybe that was because we'd broken our pattern for the day and gone farther than our norm. Seventeen of us were around the table that night: five from Brazil, four from France, three from Canada, three from Germany, and one each from Lithuania and Spain. It was the first time we encountered pilgrims from Brazil (one woman and four men). This was also the largest group of French people we had met, four bon vivants, who were having a great time together doing this section for a two-week stint. The oldest of the French travellers was seventy-four, one of the two people I met who was older than I was. The other was Ralph from California, who was a racer and a loner, in great shape, but pressing on by himself at a faster rate than most.

The wine was flowing freely and the conversation became loud and gregarious as the French and Brazilians competed for who was having the better time. Fun to watch. Jacob and I were sitting in the midst of the Brazilian contingent and received generous praise for our relationship. The other Canadian that night was Ken from Saskatoon, who was walking El Camino for the third time. He admitted to me later that he just couldn't recapture the same social life at home that he enjoyed on the walk. My first reaction was *Get a life*, but then I realized that introverts can find themselves in Spain where one and all are enduring the same challenge and welcoming every fellow pilgrim they meet. The Way is a great equalizer, where ego parks itself at the airport, at least for most. Some are starved for the special feeling they achieve and come back for more. Apparently, Ken had met a fellow who was walking the trail for the tenth time, obsessive and just a little sad that he couldn't make the same social connections back home. Ken was deeply involved in the conversation that night. The Spaniard was on the peripheral, but stayed involved, seemingly captivated by the Brazilians, while the Lithuanian and the two Germans kept to themselves at one end of the table. The rest of us engaged in lively debate, with lighthearted sarcasm playing a role.

The meal itself was another delicious paella, this time with seafood and rice, plus generous bowls of salad from freshly picked vegetables, followed by a delightful chocolate cheesecake topped with chocolate sauce and accompanied by more wine. After dessert, fatigue set in. The air went out of our collective balloons and the party, such as it was, broke up. Nine o'clock is more like midnight on the Camino. The next morning, we slept in, only to find that most of the others had left. We enjoyed a rare breakfast buffet before we left to the enduring "Buen Camino" send-off. Maybe that was our most memorable communal dinner, with the most serious competition coming from the one at Orisson on our first night. That first one had been congenial and friendly but less effusive. The second was lively and spirited, stimulated by friendly competition and better food. Hard to choose between the two.

DINNERS OF THE CAMINO

39
THE REUNION AT ASTORGA

Our next stop was Astorga, one of my favourites, with a population of about 12,000. Not a city but a nice town, large enough to offer good alternatives for both accommodation and restaurants. As mentioned, this was an unexpected joyous occasion. Jacob and I arrived in late afternoon and were standing outside a restaurant looking at the menu when we heard a yelp of elation and who should arrive but Teresa and Kathy, the Australian teachers who we'd met at breakfast on the first day. For the first week or so we met often, during the day on the trail or at a café or once or twice for dinner. The hospital incident had separated us. We hadn't seen them since, almost two weeks before. Hugs were shared. Common bonds make for quick friendships.

They had heard about me being hospitalized but nothing else. Rumours do circulate and the question "Whatever happened to…" is often repeated. I suppose we had been one of those "whatevers" for a while after we disappeared into an ambulance. It turned out that that day, our Day 25, which was October 16, was Kathy's birthday. Both ladies were now fifty-six. They joined us for supper so we celebrated together, talking for a long time, bringing each other up on the past two weeks. They thought we might have gone home and were really pleased to see us. Fortunately, Jacob's ever-present flamboyant shirt had caught their attention from a distance or we may have missed them. I can't remember the other details of our conversation, but it was quite animated, as catch-up meetings can be.

What I remember most was that they were excited that Jacob was coming to Australia and would be in Sydney at Christmas. Plans were discussed on how they would meet while addresses and phone numbers were exchanged. I was slightly envious that I would miss that second reunion. This is when Kathy astounded me by making the most generous offer to Jacob. He could use her house over the Christmas break as she would be away. Teresa invited him to have dinner at her house.

This weird and wonderful happening speaks volumes about Australian hospitality, the close relationships forged on the Way, and, most pleasing to me, the trust that Jacob had built up through his helpful nature and beaming personality. I was proud of him and grateful to these two teachers, who recognized the good heart he possesses.

40

DE NARANJA, CAFÉ CON LECHE, Y NAPOLITANA

I'm not sure I've done justice to the importance of the cafés in our daily experience. Brierley did a great job of detailing the cafés ahead for the following stretch. Our usual plan revolved around them for our much-needed breaks as well as selecting the albergue to which we'd send the black bag. I cannot adequately explain the joy of seeing the selected café ahead, knowing that a short rest was imminent and we were about to reach one of the day's landmarks.

These quite unpretentious meeting places offered shelter on a rainy day, warmth on a cold day, conversation and comfort on every day, and to quote from the musical *Oliver*, food glorious food. I mentioned earlier that I had to boost my calorie intake or risk other health issues. I had been losing weight too fast and lacked energy. I also had to increase my liquid intake or risk dehydration. The solution was provided by the cafés. Most of them were stocked from local bakeries. Fresh bread was always available. But more enticing were the napolitanas, which were available almost everywhere. These are freshly baked, oversized, chocolate croissants served warm, oozing with melted chocolate. Calories plus. Increasing the liquids was easy. Drink more water and enjoy a café con leche, the Spanish equivalent of a café au lait, plus a large glass of freshly squeezed orange juice.

No matter how small the establishment, these basic roadside stopovers were able to come through. On a good day we would start with this glorious trio for breakfast before leaving and have not one but two stops, repeating the same selections before lunch. That's right, three chocolate croissants before noon. I estimated I was eating at least six thousand calories a day and not gaining an ounce.

On the colder days when we were back up in the mountains, the joy of the café included a small fire adding to the warmth and comfort of the stop. A simple life with simple comforts. Is there anything better? At the time, I didn't think so.

41
THE CROSS AND THE STONE

Each would-be pilgrim is instructed to bring a stone from home to deposit at the Cruz de Ferro, which is located partway through Stage 24, between Rabanal del Camino and Molinaseca. While it sits at the highest point in that area at about five thousand feet, in the midst of a splendid natural site, the cross itself is very basic: a simple iron cross mounted on a well-weathered wooden pole. The site was not at all what I expected. In fact, I admit I was disappointed. The base of the cross was piled high with stones in quite a wide circle around the base, which I presumed were deposited by pilgrims over the past fifty years, since the beginning of the modern Camino. Regardless of its significance, the untidy pile of assorted stones looked shoddy to me, more like a garbage dump than a holy site, diminished even further by a foggy damp Day 27.

I had carefully selected a nice granite rock from my cottage in Muskoka. Forgetting what was ahead that day, it was in transit with my black bag. Jacob had his stone with him and carefully worked his way up the misshapen pile to set it at the base of the wooden standard. I'm not sure where he got his stone or if it had a special meaning to him. We never discussed that. Leaving your chosen talisman symbolizes that you are leaving all your burdens behind. Not a bad idea two-thirds of the way through a challenging journey. I suppose my burdens and worries had to stay with me because I still carried my stone, sort of. Legend says that the cross was placed in this location in the eleventh century, which means travellers began leaving their stones and their burdens there for the past thousand years, much earlier than I had thought. After seeing so many beautiful cathedrals and churches, this site just didn't resonate with me. Instead, the unsightly pile of mixed rocks detracted from the natural beauty. To me, that symbolized man's uncanny ability to damage nature. To each his own.

I understand that all places of religious significance need not be grandiose or ostentatious. The cathedrals were built to the glory of God and could never do justice to that purpose, no matter how ornate. Instead, the glory that I perceived was the natural beauty and the breathtaking view. To a less religious fellow, the location seemed more suited to its original use for pagan worship before it was converted for a Christian purpose. There were not many people at the site when we were there. Some approached the base of the cross reverently. Jacob was one of those, although oddly, we never discussed why or how he felt in the process. I walked carefully around the circle of stone surrounding the cross and waited for him on the other side. It was the only time along the Way that I was underwhelmed by a monument. I'm sure that I am in the minority. You will have to go and see for yourself. As for my rock and I suppose my burdens, they stayed with me for the rest of the journey.

42
NO FOOL LIKE AN OLD FOOL

The end of each day was the most difficult time throughout my Camino. I often thought of the Irish ladies as the afternoon passed by, for those last Spanish kilometres, without fail, seemed much longer than any of those I had walked back in Canada in my attempt to prepare.

The afternoon after we passed the Cruz de Ferro, I gave in to temptation. We stopped for a relaxed lunch about ten kilometres away from our goal in Molinaseca. We were facing our steepest, long descent of our Camino, roughly nine hundred metres down on a slope that, on average, was a nine percent decline. Pretty steep. As I've said, I found the sudden descents difficult. Often, we had to pick our way down steep rocky paths. When we did, my knees ached constantly as I used my walking sticks for stability as well as to take a load off my legs. The chances of tripping and having a fall were much worse than anything you faced on the way up.

At lunch we met a German fellow who was walking the Camino for the fourth time. He made no bones about the next stage: he detested it. He was considering taking a lift to the next town, skipping the descent completely, and insisted that I would be better off to avoid the rugged trail down. Instead, he recommended walking the road, which meandered back and forth across the mountainous route at much gentler declines. It would be a longer walk but much easier.

Jacob was not interested. An easier way was never interesting to Jake. That would be cheating. Normally I would have agreed, but that afternoon I made a stubborn, foolish decision. If he wouldn't come with me, I would go it alone and meet him at our albergue. Big mistake.

That was the *only* time we separated on the trail. At first, I felt vindicated. Walking on the side of the road was safe and, for sure, easier on the knees. There were few cars. In fact, for the next three hours I only saw one and that was early on. There were no pilgrims. No cyclists. No buses. Nothing. Just me and what soon became a boring paved road. As the roads twisted and turned, I reached a fork in the road. Which way to go? I picked what I thought was right, but as I worked my way slowly downwards, I remembered the Korean lady who had picked the wrong way and we never saw her again. Was that going to be me?

Regardless, this solo walk was a lonely experience, even more so with doubt closing in after an hour on my own. I began to wish that a car would come along to validate my choice and let me confirm I was heading in the right direction. None came.

I was definitely missing Jake and his complete sense of confidence as we found our way. I began to realize that I relied more on his common-sense approach and his bush experience than I thought. Tree planters spend a fair amount of time in isolation, dropped off to plant in their own sector, visited once or twice a day by their group leader. He was used to that feeling. I did not like the sense of being so secluded, possibly lost, in a foreign country. I had sent my phone ahead in the black bag because we relied on Jacob's phone for information and outside contact during the day. I would have loved to be able to call him. The day was winding down as we were well into fall by this point. What was I going to do?

By that time, tears were welling up, but I'll never admit it to Jacob, unless he happens to read this later. Even then I'll likely say I only added that idea to our story for dramatic effect. Believe what you will. I'm the only one who knows for sure what I was feeling. Finally, as I was at my lowest point, I heard a faint voice from well above me. "Hey, Gramps, how's it going?"

Jake was about three hundred feet above me and about fifty metres ahead. "The village is just around the next bend, you're only a few hundred yards away." Wow! What a relief! I had just enough time to collect myself before he joined me, just as we turned that corner. I hugged him, tighter than normal, but I don't think he noticed.

When he asked how my afternoon went, I said, "Great, how was yours?" His response warmed my heart. "It was fine, but I think we should stick together from now on." I couldn't have agreed more.

43

THE MOST BEAUTIFUL FALL DAY—LA VIE EN ROSE

We'd set out from Saint-Jean-Pied-de-Port on September 22 fully expecting fall-like weather with mild temperatures, mainly sunny days, and perhaps rain about thirty percent of the time. Instead, as I've mentioned, we had summer-like heat with temperatures in the mid-thirties Celsius for the first week, later the high twenties Celsius in the last week, and a few days at two to five degrees Celsius in the middle. We had exactly one typical lovely fall day so far, and this was it.

The countdown had continued and we had approximately two hundred and fifteen kilometres left when we started out that morning. The next two stages totalled just under sixty kilometres, with the second one including the largest climb we would make on a single day: over nine hundred metres. These were tough back-to-back hikes. Sending the black bag thirty kilometres ahead for each was one hell of a commitment but we had no choice. We didn't want to lose any more time. We hoped to spend three days in Santiago, another to visit Finnisterre, and one last one in Barcelona before flying home on Day 42. That left us nine days to complete the remaining nine stages.

This first stage of the two was relatively flat, but it was important to cover as much ground as possible to shorten the second day if we could. We were anticipating a long demanding walk, but nature did us a favour and served up the nicest weather of our Camino: a stunning fall day with the sun shining and a cool but not cold temperature—a perfect setting for an energetic hike. The day was memorable for more than the weather. For whatever reason, the two of us were on our own almost the entire day. There were numerous small windows like this over the six weeks where we were by ourselves but never for such an extended number of hours. The time flew by as we discussed the present, the future, and the past. Of the thousand-plus hours we spent together, on our adventure, these were among the best. But we didn't always talk. Sometimes we walked in silence, which for me meant thinking of many things, whether it be fantasizing about my place had I been in involved in one of the many historical periods of the region or simply thinking of my wife and what she might be doing at home. The actual thoughts and the conversation that day are a blur. My journal says little beyond "perfect day."

What I do remember about that dream day was walking along the side of a river for a few hours. I can't conjure up a lot of details, but I can recapture the feeling of total freedom. No burdens on my shoulders, whether real or imagined. The initial part of the path was downhill, the rest of the way was quite flat, with a slight uphill at the end. Dare I say a stress-free easy walk in the park? Perhaps the best way to define that moment in time was through the music that kept playing in my head that day. The song was "La Vie en Rose" by Edith Piaf—perhaps the most defining song of her illustrious career. The English meaning, not quite literally, but actually, is "seeing life through rose-coloured glasses," which means seeing the best in everything. The English words are quite beautiful but in French, that song, *c'est magnifique!* Why do romantic songs sound so much better in French? That tune became my anthem for that day and for the rest of the trip.

As we walked together in silence, I felt my love for Jacob, for my wife, Karin, for my entire family, for life itself, and for the simple pleasures of a glorious day walking with my grandson in perfect weather. That night, we arrived later than planned. Thirty kilometres is still thirty kilometres. We didn't rush because it wasn't necessary. We had sent the black bag to the first albergue in the village but were surprised that we were the only ones staying there. The albergue itself was one of the least memorable. Our experience was rather strange. Choices were minimal, leading to one of the worst meals of the entire trip. No substantial food was presented so we dined on potato chips, chocolate bars, and Coke Zero. Junk food city. No conversation was offered or welcomed. The pervading feeling was loneliness and isolation, belying the uplifting day we had just completed. Weird and unusual for the Camino. However, most important, the black bag was waiting for us and those earlier hours, feeling so much at ease, had been simply magical. Tired, I fell into bed, as contented as I'd been the entire trip, but Brierley reminded me that things were about to change.

44
O'CEBRIERO

My good friend John was right! Deservedly, he and I were now on a first-name basis, even though he didn't know it; after all, I read him every night. I even had the odd animated conversation with him when I felt he'd led us astray, but most of the time I believed him. The most challenging day of the entire Camino came on this day, our Day 29, which was Stage 26 of the 33 Stages that Brierley outlined in his guidebook. He describes this stage as "strenuous, particularly at the end, one of the steepest of the entire pilgrimage, but rewarded with stunning views." A mixed blessing at best, but a grim reminder that our challenge was back in full force after a brief reprieve.

The pattern of the path magnified the intensity of the pain and the challenge. To summarize what was ahead as strenuous, where we would climb over nine hundred metres, proved to be an understatement. First, we climbed five hundred, then descended over two hundred, before re-climbing two hundred, then descending roughly three hundred, and finishing with a six-hundred-metre climb. If you add the total up, we climbed thirteen hundred metres to reach our final destination. The final six hundred ascended came in the last eight kilometres of a twenty-eight-kilometre hike under some pretty rough terrain. That's an average 7.5 percent incline for close to three hours. That's runaway-truck territory when it lasts that long, but it's hell on earth four weeks into a demanding walk at the end of the day!

The powers that be, those who created this world, have their own unique sense of humour. On the golf course, it's reflected in the triple bogey you have on the last hole of your best round ever. Or the birdie you have on that same last whole at the end of your worst round ever. Whatever, this exhausting part of the journey was the antithesis of the previous day. My senses were numb. There was little time to talk, no time to imagine anything. Every step required concentration and effort. You might think that the downward parts would compensate, but they don't. El Camino establishes early on that the descent over rough terrain can be more difficult than going up. All of this was accomplished as the temperature significantly declined. It could have been worse. It could have rained as it did the next day. For a different reason, like the previous stage, I remember few details, but I do remember my overall feeling. This was the only day where I thought yet again, *I can't do this!*

But I did, encouraged by Jacob all the way but especially during the steepest stretches. And God, the Creator, or Nature, whatever your belief, did not disappoint. The good followed the bad. My worst day was well rewarded when we reached our destination at O'Cebreiro, a tiny mountain village, perched on the edge of the summit, with a spectacular view of the valley below and the path we had just completed. Literally, this was one of the high points of the trip. A location that has been welcoming pilgrims for well over a thousand years. We had just crossed from the state of Léon into Galicia, the last of the four states on our journey. We were sitting one hundred and fifty-five kilometres and seven days from our goal.

Our albergue sat right on the edge, highlighting the view and leaving me in wonderment of the climb just completed. While I collapsed into my bunk, Jacob explored, wandering around the top of his most recent conquest. I was less sure who had won the day: me or the mountain. He soon returned with a Camino patch, which he quickly sewed onto his backpack. His tattoo had healed so another, less enduring souvenir seemed appropriate. The challenging climb that almost defeated me had merely rebooted his elation. On that day, a mere thirteen hundred metres above sea level, it felt like the top of the world. The Camino is full of personal victories: those of the average, who never do the impossible; and those like Jacob, for which there are few limits. That night is a blur. I don't recall the dinner at all. I might even have slept from my late-afternoon nap right through to morning.

We started out the next day walking in the clouds as rain and cold set in. The temperature was two degrees Celsius. I spent the entire morning taking my rain jacket off because I was hot and putting it back on because I was wet. The rain persisted past lunch, but the sun came out as we descended about seven hundred metres that afternoon. At times the days do run together, and those two days after O'Cebriero definitely did. They left me with feeling of drudgery and dampness. We marshalled on through the most unpleasant weather of the entire trip: cold, wet, and misty. Santiago still seemed far away but it really wasn't. We were getting close to where the marshmallow tourist-type pilgrims would join us for the last one hundred kilometres to claim their ill-deserved Compostela.

On the second day, the rain was accompanied by high winds—the only time I got really soaked. Fortunately, my shoes didn't. They never did. The second napolitana of the day was greatly appreciated when we stopped at a café that had a lovely warm fire burning in a traditional stone fireplace. I was in no hurry to leave and noticed a few other *peregrinos* who felt the same. Onward we went, though. The terrain was less demanding but the conditions weren't great. Both days were relatively short distances as we covered thirty-nine kilometres in total, almost all in a soggy environment. At the end of the second day, we reached Sarria. I learned so much about the Camino and its tourist side after we reached Sarria, but you'll have to wait to find out what.

45
WEE FEE

You're probably thinking I'm going to write about a small bill, literally a "wee fee." Not so—this is about something far more important. You would recognize the title if it was the proper trademarked form rather than the Spanish pronunciation. Or at least that's the way most albergue managers pronounced Wi-Fi, if they offered it (most do, but not all).

The relative importance of this oft taken-for-granted service clearly defines the age gap between Jacob and me. The younger generation depends heavily on the free Internet access it provides. They are far more aware of the costs of using expensive cellular minutes. On the Camino, Wi-Fi brings unlimited Internet access and WhatsApp free calling, most importantly long distance. For Jacob it was a lifeline, a tie to knowledge, answers to many questions, and phone and text access to his girlfriend, who was completing a university semester in Perth, Australia. I had no hesitation in using my cellular plan to call my wife any time I needed to talk with her. I admit, I did enjoy the free Wi-Fi for emailing and reading my Apple News.

For Jacob, no Wi-Fi simply meant walking to the next café during the day and to the next albergue in the late afternoon without hesitation. Not that simple for me. Happily, that rarely happened in 2016 and probably even less so today. However, it did happen once and caused us to add an extra three kilometres to our walk that afternoon. Naturally, adding three kilometres during my end-of-the-day struggles wasn't popular with the old guy and my alter ego, Grumps, reappeared immediately. The thought of picking up the black bag and having to carry it for an uncertain distance had zero appeal to me. I suppose Jacob saw me wince because he picked up the bag like it was feather weight, which it wasn't, and strode off, disgusted that in this day and age he was being denied one of life's basic needs. He wasn't wasting time. He needed that Wi-Fi. Soon he was a few hundred yards ahead as I dragged my butt along. The good news was that I would have to walk less the next day and Gramps soon returned. I suppose that is where our world is headed. Vulnerability to our source of connection is a serious threat. Without the Internet, we are crippled. It just didn't seem that important in the midst of a pilgrimage. But it was to anyone under the age of thirty.

There were a few other age-related differences. I needed water far more than alcohol. Neither of us drank much, but it was easy for me to avoid any after-dinner drinks. We met enough younger people for Jacob to go out after we ate and enjoy a glass of wine or a beer or two. He did this occasionally while I was reading Brierley. I also used that time to compose my poems to Karin and write emails until lights out at 10:00 p.m. I was asleep almost immediately, but Jake was awake for hours into the night communicating with Australia and Canada. Thank God for Wee Fee.

Beyond that, I did my laundry more than he did. I ate less. I walked slower. I may have snored more, but I don't think so. He used his Spanish more—no inhibitions about that. I was in the hospital more. Once and a while he ran a bit. I *never* ran. He carried a saxophone. I had no musical instrument with me but couldn't play one if I had. Beyond that, we were like two peas in a pod, one of us slightly more wrinkled than the other. Dehydration? Regrettably, not. Oh yes, another age difference, appearance—old guy and young guy—but that just didn't matter.

SITES AND SCENES FROM OUR CAMINO

46
CAMINO SHORTS

Quite a few of our Camino tales are more like observations and don't require the full-scale anecdote treatment. I think they're still interesting so here are a few:

1. One day as we walked past a golf course, we saw a sign welcoming *peregrinos* for lunch. Unusual on a Sunday afternoon to invite a scraggly bunch of pilgrims into your dining room. At first, we hesitated, but as we apprehensively approached the entrance, we were greeted warmly and then served lunch after choosing from quite an extensive menu. Jacob was determined to hit a few balls on a Spanish course for future bragging rights. We lobbied hard to go out to their driving range. I actually thought they might let us, but we were told politely that it was a private club so no way. Maybe the dress code did us in. We were okay to buy a lunch but that was it. I don't know why but hitting a few golf balls in Spain was appealing to both of us.

2. We were quite taken by the wide variety of trees we observed during our Camino. The most surprising were the eucalyptus trees we saw in Galicia during the last week of our walk. Apparently, in the nineteenth century, a Galician monk planted seeds he had brought back

from Australia. The trees spread extensively across the area and have been used broadly in the timber and pulp industries. But we didn't see a single koala. Apparently, they don't grow from seeds. Other species we encountered (and I'm sure there were more) included olive, oak, red pine, spruce, balsam, chestnut, walnut, maple, palm, apple, pear, kiwi, and fig. A girl from Israel introduced Jacob and me to fig trees, growing wild, and convinced us to try the fruit. Delicious and most welcome in the heat of our first few days.

3. On Day 26, we arrived at a very proper *donativo* albergue, run by an English couple. Tea and cake were served promptly at 4:30 p.m., a small taste of Britain. Then we adjourned to a lovely fireside library, with an extensive collection of non-fiction books, in both English and Spanish. Appropriately that's where I wrote my journal entry of the day. I do love books. The setting was quite formal and I was sitting at a large walnut desk in an extremely comfortable leather chair. Britain comes to Spain, so to speak. Dickens shoved Cervantes aside for a night. Jacob sat in the corner looking less comfortable on a small settee but content, making full use of the Wi-Fi. The books didn't distract him from his phone.

4. When we were staying in O'Cebriero, I had a short conversation just before lights out with Theresa from the UK. She was a racer, having completed what took us twenty-nine days in eighteen days. Our conversation became very emotional, and I believe she opened up to me because I was an older man. Her father had died a short time before and she had terrible regrets about her relationship with him. She was using the Way as penance, punishing herself severely by walking so intently, ultimately seeking atonement, I presume. Theresa was the only pilgrim I talked with who derived no pleasure in the effort. Her goal was misery. Sad but true.

5. One concern about walking the Camino was the rumour about bedbugs. Karin and I had acquired some permethrin from Buffalo, New York, as we couldn't find any in Canada. Jacob and I dutifully sprayed the exterior of our sleeping bags and backpacks as a precaution. Good news: I didn't hear about one issue concerning bedbugs. In addition, there was a firm rule that if an albergue found bedbugs it had to close until they were eliminated. The paper pillowcase and

bottom sheets handed out on check-in were destroyed each day to minimize any chance of spreading the parasites.

6. One day just after we'd crossed an old medieval bridge and entered into a village, we were held back for a while as a local parade moved through. It was an unusual parade, featuring what appeared to be bagpipes and some locals dressed in kilts. The pipes were recognizable but the tunes were not. No "Scotland the Brave" that day. We had no idea what we were seeing, but it was distinctively different so we made note of it to ask later. Apparently, the instrument we saw is called the *gaita* and is used today at festivals whose origins date back hundreds of years to a Celtic people who settled in Galicia and other parts of north east Spain—and they do wear kilt-like garments.

7. This still bothers me. Why do all the dormitories have such high ceilings but such low bunk beds that tired people keep hitting their heads on? Things that go bump in the night (see #11 below).

8. The first day after we left Sarria, I found myself walking beside a fellow from Barcelona whose name was Francisco. I've mentioned him earlier. He'd had a hip replacement about six months before, and we had quite a bit in common as he was close to my age and well read on a variety of topics. We had extensive conversations over those last days of our trek, from health to politics to everything in between. He was a proud Catalonian who strongly supported separation from Spain. When he found out I was Canadian, he began asking a wide range of questions about the separation referendums in Quebec. He was well versed about what had happened in Canada and was keen to know how I felt about it. He explained that the Catalonian independence movement was a hundred years in the making but had gained a resurgence in the past decade. He was passionate in his support. I enjoyed his company. The last time I saw him was on the day we arrived in Santiago at the Pilgrims Office, where we all got our Compostela.

9. Some comparative statistics: Walking the eight hundred kilometres on the Camino is approximately equivalent to walking from Toronto to Quebec City, or Detroit to New York, or Boston to Cleveland. The distance that took us thirty-six days to walk can be covered in a car on good highways in eight hours or in an airplane

in just over an hour. But both of these options include no significant experience and zero local exposure.

10. Another experience in Galicia was walking through an area with an abundance of heather and scotch broom on the sides of the trail. Heather has a pretty flower, while scotch broom, an undesirable weed-like plant, aggressively chokes out most anything else. For a short while on that rainy day, we could have been in Scotland.

11. Dormitory living is an adjustment, one of a number that are easier to make at twenty-two than at seventy-one. If you do make your Camino, be sure to bring earplugs. Otherwise, the guaranteed symphony of snores, accentuated occasionally by flatulence, will disrupt your much needed sleep. Every albergue is laid out a little differently. Get a bunk against a wall if you can. One night in our first week, when we were still learning the ropes, we got in a bit late and had no choice. We were stuck in one of the last empty bunks in the middle of a large room where the bunks were arranged row on row. Even worse, only top bunks were available. That was the only night I slept on top. The fellow in the neighbouring bunk was a Spaniard who spoke little English and showed no interest in conversation. However, about every half-hour all night long, he sat up and spewed out two or three rapid sentences in Spanish, never waking up. Then he would lay back down and resume his sleep, leaving me wide awake waiting for the next outburst. Not ideal after a tiring day.

That's enough Camino shorts for now. Naturally there's more, but these few provide a little more detail and an added touch of the flavour of our travels. Time to revisit Sarria.

47
SARRIA

The path leading into Sarria was a shorter eighteen kilometres so we extended it by walking right through to the other side of this town of about 14,000 inhabitants. In doing so, we passed several albergues, which is why the one we finally chose was empty. Jacob had to carry the black bag through town because we'd sent it to one of the first albergues. The weather was cold and when we finally arrived the most welcome heat was on. Sarria has become a focal point for the modern Camino. My image of the Camino was doing the complete eight hundred kilometres in one attempt, or even farther by following the old pilgrim routes starting much farther away. The movie The Way portrayed that image of one complete walk. I'd already been disillusioned by the bikers, the buses, and the Europeans who did their pilgrimage one or two weeks at a time over several years. None of this remotely replicated the suffering and effort experienced by those original medieval pilgrims. Theirs was the experience I was seeking.

Sarria is an old town with somewhat of a Celtic history. Many of those medieval travellers stopped there. However, it seems that the lure of modern tourism and the money that flows into Spain from it has led the organizers of the Camino to change the rules. As I've revealed, I was crushed to find out that if one walks at least one hundred kilometres, meaning starting in Sarria, then that person receives the same Compostela that I was going to receive for starting in Saint-Jean. Blasphemy! That change diminishes the accomplishment and belittles the effort it takes, making a gross misrepresentation of what a serious pilgrimage involves. To be sure, we can never replicate the struggles, threats, and difficulty experienced by pilgrims a thousand years ago. Modern conveniences like cafés every few kilometres, Brierley's guidebook, albergues in every town or village, and pilgrim specials in every restaurant ensure that. But at least we were walking in their shoes along terrain that was often unchanged. Over the next few days, I saw additional signs of catering to tourists who, as you know by now, I classify as pseudo-pilgrims. In some areas the path is wider, even graded. As a businessman I get it, but in the chase for dollars something is being lost. Not completely but to a significant degree. The experience of walking from Sarria would not warrant a book. Maybe a newspaper column or two. Jacob mirrored my disappointment but I reassured him: nothing could take away from this marvellous shared experience. That's it—rant finished.

For almost three hours we had the large room in that albergue to ourselves. Between about 8:30 and 9:00 p.m., two bigger groups arrived. Both were just starting their mini-Caminos. I labelled the first group "The Ladies of Spain," as a parody of the old song. These seven young women were in a party mood, taking a few days off to *earn* their Compostela. Within a few minutes a second group arrived: six relatively young Italian men with the same limited commitment. Great.

Soon both groups were mingling outside on the patio, and the marijuana was circulating. Definitely a different crowd and not at all interested in the old guy already nestled in his sleeping bag. Jacob went out and talked to them for a half-hour but decided not to partake. I would have understood had he stayed out, but I was glad to have him come back in and settle down for the night. We saw those ladies a few times over the next week, always chattering away and giggling. Don't get me wrong, young people should be carefree, happy, and partying when they can. Not hard to do when the walks are shorter and the path is less demanding.

The next day as we left, we saw a sign outside of town that read, *Christ did not start in Sarria.* It made me laugh, realizing that I was reacting far too seriously. I have no claim to being a Camino purist. That said, Christ did not even walk in Spain but, according to legend, Saint James did, and he certainly would not have taken the short easy road. Why? *Because it didn't exist!* This change in the Camino is a reflection of our society's preoccupation with making things easier, but doesn't that tendency tend to weaken our collective resolve? The intent to restore the Camino pilgrimage was a test. Not a tour.

48
THE FOREVER DAYS

Only five days left. The countdown showed just over one hundred kilometres ahead. Five shorter days, averaging about twenty kilometres. Easy, right? Physically, that should be true. Mentally, not so much. Our routine remained the same. With the influx of new people, conversations on the trail were fresh and different. Jacob was still a magnet to meet people and he was loving the additional contact. I should have been beaming with exuberance—I was going to make it—but I wasn't. Santiago was the carrot and I was the donkey. The days passed slowly and our pace matched the feeling.

These were the days when I coined the phrase *Better than Brierley*. His projected distances had to be off. The walks seemed longer. The climbs seemed higher. The physical challenge was largely over, but it had turned into a psychological one. We probably stopped more often for longer. The end of the trip ranked right up there with the end of the day. The weather had returned to summer-like, with temperatures around twenty-seven or twenty-eight degrees Celsius. Maybe the return to heat slowed us down. Maybe the certainty of getting there took away the urgency to press ahead. Maybe the thought of going home reminded me of the separation from Karin. Maybe. Maybe. Maybe.

I tried not to show it because Jacob was far more upbeat, but I often lagged behind while he walked with a young man his own age, Marc, also from Barcelona. I particularly remember the walk into Portomarín. It started out as our second beautiful fall day of the trip. Toward the end, though, we had a taste of the first stages again, with a walk down a rocky, narrow, steep slope. It wasn't long, but it was right at the end of the day.

Portomarín was a very awkward town, at least in terms of access. First, we had to cross a long bridge over the River Mino to get into town. We would have to cross back to continue the next day to resume on the trail. It was the only time we didn't just walk through the town. This was an unwelcome diversion, which ended by us walking up what seemed like a hundred steps or more to get into the town and our albergue. That day seemed like it would never end. Grumps was back. That night, we just walked to a close-by *supermercado* and ate inside the albergue.

The next three days were similar, particularly at the end of the day when I was dragging my butt. My drive was simply diminished, my willpower waning. The shorter distances didn't make a difference. The countdown sluggishly approached zero. The next night we went to another *supermercado*. I knew I wasn't eating well and yet another *peregrino* roasted chicken dinner wasn't that tempting. My conversations with Francisco helped.

Then we met up with Theresa and Kathy again. Kathy had twisted her ankle and was limping badly. They had stopped early that night and we wondered if she'd be able to finish. We also met a French woman, Ovietta, who was struggling as well, using a cane. Travelling by herself, she was close to giving up and taking a bus back to Avignon in France. We walked with her for quite a while on the second day, trying to encourage her, and then she disappeared. We presumed she went home.

Seeing these very real problems of others revitalized my determination. It was fruitless to come this far and not finish. That's when we met Ralph, the seventy-eight-year-old American sprinter who ended up completing his Camino in twenty days. He was walking alone, which I believe accounted for his speedwalking. He didn't take the time to socialize. He just hustled along. Regardless, there was no way I could let this older guy steamroll by without catching his vibe. Even if I kept it to myself, what was I complaining about? Enough of this negativity. I rebooted and was ready to finish on a high note. Grumps rescinded and Gramps was back. Luckily Jacob had hardly noticed.

49
OCTOPUS AND A BURGER

That third day, as things were looking up, we planned to indulge ourselves with a gourmet lunch, enjoyed at our leisure. The distance that day was a little longer, just over twenty-five kilometres, but we'd had an early start. When we reached Melide, we started looking for a nice place to eat. The midday countdown indicated just fifty more kilometres ahead.

As it turned out, we had to walk practically right through the town, climbing a fair-sized hill in the process, before we found an interesting restaurant. When we did, we quickly picked out what we hoped would be that much anticipated gourmet lunch. At least it seemed gourmet after days of chicken, salad, tortillas, and rice. To be sure, the food was always good, but a change was overdue and certainly tempting. One of the redeeming features of Galicia is that it borders the Cantabrian Sea to the north and the Atlantic Ocean to the west. A major sector of its economy is fishing. That meant lots of seafood options. Jacob had been reading up and was intrigued with the delicacies involving the octopus, which were native to the area.

He saw exactly what he wanted: a huge bowl of purply edged octopus. Pulpo a la Gallega was one of the region's defining dishes, and it had been boiled in the local tradition. He'd done his research, sharing with me that octopus is low in fat, high in iron, and significantly more tender than its squid cousin calamari. Jacob was set, but what would I choose? I wasn't that interested in the octopus. After reviewing the menu at length, I made the safe choice for something I hadn't eaten in two months: the ever-popular Angus burger, Galician-style but fundamentally exactly what you would expect, including French fries. We had seen little or no beef along the Way and definitely no fries. According to Jake, the octopus was delicious, sort of like chicken but sweeter. I tried a sampling and he was right. As for the burger, when you haven't had one for a while it tasted excellent. Both items came with a typical Spanish salad made from the freshest of vegetables, topped up with a glass of wine for me and a beer for Jake. No *peregrino* dinner for us that day. Such indulgence.

We left the restaurant at 2:30 p.m. and still had ten kilometres to go that day. The rest of the afternoon dragged a bit, but our spirits were up so that didn't matter. There was lots of chatter about the meal, about the distance left to Santiago, about our plans when we got there, about his going to Australia a few days after we got back to Canada, and so on. Happy talk. A good day all around at just the time it was needed. It was almost 6:00 p.m. by the time we arrived at our albergue. Our black bag was waiting and Wee Fee was available. Life was good—simple and good. We were both so satiated that we skipped dinner. The countdown was now at forty-two kilometres. We had tasted octopus, and now we could taste the end of the trail.

50
WHEN DOES THE MAN BECOME THE CHILD?

I had set out on this journey hoping to help Jacob find himself. To deal with his few demons, his limited anxieties, which we all have, and help him get on a solid path to the future I hoped for him. In my mind he was still the boy on the verge of becoming a man, with so many decisions ahead. I was the elder, the man with the wisdom tempered by years of experience. My second goal was to understand him better as I got to know him more intimately with all the time spent together. That ambition was attained, and I think it worked both ways.

What I hadn't realized is that the Camino experience helps everyone understand themselves better. It helps you view the world differently. That was an unexpected side effect. I entered the journey thinking of myself as the adult of our duo. Jacob had never been to Europe. I had several times on business and with Karin on vacation. But those last few days when I was struggling with the forever days, I understood that something had changed. The boy who had lost his hat and his watch on the flight over had taken a leap forward into the helpful young man liked by everyone we met. Instead, I was the one who needed encouragement. The entrepreneur in me was not the one leading the charge to make things happen. It was the entrepreneur-to-be who was pushing the envelope and leading us both toward our goal.

It was that young man whom I found out had waited patiently, watching over me from above, when I insisted on taking the road instead of staying with him. It was that young man who had raced back to the albergue and grabbed all of our gear when I was being shoved into an ambulance. The same guy who called his Nana to reassure her and get a list of my medications for the hospital staff. It was that young man who said, "Don't worry, Nana, I'll take care of him." It was that young man who carried our large heavy black bag when necessary. The young man in the bunk above me could be counted on. The elder encouraged entrepreneurship and recited many facets of that mindset. At times, the student sometimes became the teacher, filling in the old guy about WhatsApp and meditation. The protector was slowly becoming the protected. How great was that.

Mutual understanding became one of the key by-products of our Camino. To be sure, there were many challenges ahead. That hopeful future path was still a few years away. Missteps were inevitable. Setbacks would happen. But the combination of a good heart and a good mind would prevail in the end. As we walked the Camino, I knew with more certainty that the maturation process would continue aided by the strong bond we had forged. The torch was in the process of being passed. The young man still had lots to learn and the old man could help but realized he could still learn as well. The wisdom would always be there to share, but that would only happen when requested. As you get older the body starts to slip, but if you're lucky the mind persists. I can always count on Jacob for physical help and emotional support. However, when *does* the old man become the boy again?

51
HELP FROM AFAR

Being away with Jacob was a great experience from the get-go. But leaving my wife, Karin, for six weeks was a first, after forty-nine years of marriage. While we were on an exciting adventure, Karin was left at home on her own, albeit with the support of family and friends. She did break up her time alone by visiting our son Rob and his family in Vancouver over Thanksgiving, which I'm sure helped. At first, we only exchanged brief emails. Jacob and I were busy travelling to get there, chasing down lost luggage, and just adjusting to our new reality. But, especially after Logroño and my hospital experience, she and I started exchanging longer messages. Because of the time difference, I would write at night and receive her answers in the morning. Many of her messages included a quote or a poem to encourage me. For example:

"Walking with Grandpa" by Rodney O. Hurd

I like to walk with Grandpa,
His steps are short like mine.
He doesn't say "Now hurry up!"
He always takes his time.

Most people have to hurry,
They do not stop and see.
I'm glad that God made Grandpa
"Unrushed" and young like me.

Not too bad, although I could have added:
Jacob's steps were never short,
And too often I lagged behind.
But I learned perhaps the hard way,
That my grandson is smart and kind.

Here are a few thought-provoking quotes (some anonymous) she sent relevant to my journey and the challenge that I faced:

"A journey is best measured in friends, rather than miles."

"Travel makes one modest. You see what a tiny place you occupy in the world."

"When I let go of what I am, I become what I might be."

"Happiness is found along the way—not at the end of the journey."

"Common sense and good nature will do a lot to make the pilgrimage of life not too difficult."
—Somerset Maugham

"Great things are done when men and mountains meet."
—William Blake

"The sum of the whole is this: walk and be happy; walk and be healthy."
—Charles Dickens

"Our way is not soft grass, it's a mountain pass with lots of rocks. But it goes upwards, forward, toward the sun."
—Ruth Westheimer

"The best thing one can do when it's raining is to let it rain."
—Henry Wadsworth Longfellow

"The nicest thing about the rain is that it always stops."
—A.A. Milne (Eeyore)

"Some people feel the rain. Others just get wet."
—Bob Marley

Karin also sent me a number of quotes about love. I'll share a few of the less personal ones.

"If I had a flower for every time I thought of you, I would walk through my garden forever."
—Alfred Lord Tennyson

"All you need is love. But a little chocolate now and then doesn't hurt."
—Charles M. Schulz

"Being deeply loved by someone gives you strength, while loving someone deeply gives you courage."
—Lao Tzu

"Love is but the discovery of ourselves in others and the delight in the recognition."
—Plato

That last one summed up the process between Jacob and I on our pilgrimage. Karin sent me love poems as well, some she wrote and some she quoted, and every morning I looked forward to what she sent, making for a great start to my day. I responded in kind each night. It became a little competition to try find the best quote or poem or to write one of our own. That and the twice-a-week phone calls kept us connected. That intimacy lifted me up when I was down, and I hope that it did the same for her when she felt alone. I include only this one poem of mine, which I wrote and sent from Santiago, three days before I got home:

> Home is where your heart is
> The place you feel at ease
> Where you feel true contentment
> Shared with one you love to please
>
> Home is where I'm headed
> So anxious to enter that door
> To be back with my alter ego
> The person that I so adore
>
> For home is not a building
> Not a cottage, house, or retreat
> It's wherever we're together
> Just you and I, my sweet

Our separation was great in miles, but we were always together, providing each other with help and support.

52
WE DID IT!

On Day 36 we walked into Santiago de Compostela after walking more than one million, one hundred thousand steps and spending close to a thousand hours together. Not a step was missed. We covered the entire eight hundred kilometres on foot, making us true pilgrims. We arrived in the early afternoon, experiencing a brief rain shower as we entered the city. All was forgiven.

Brierley was back in my good books, but an uneasy feeling of elation mixed with uncertainty came over me. For weeks, everything we did had been clearly defined. Now we were done. We had reached our goal. What next?

We immediately walked directly to the cathedral, where we ran into several people who we had met along the Way. The first people we recognized were the couple who had trained so thoroughly, Fred and Karen from Peterborough, whom we hadn't seen since Day 3. We'd thought they might have been as much as a week ahead of us, but they'd arrived only two days before us and were flying home the next day. Then the young Australian woman who'd had the blister problem came running over. As I mentioned in an earlier chapter, we'd seen her maybe a dozen times over the five weeks but we'd never spoken. She gave Jacob and me each a big hug and told us excitedly how neat it was that we'd travelled together. For the moment, the feeling of uncertainty had disappeared. Both Jacob and I were on an emotional high.

The next two days brought more reunions as so many connections arrived. We saw Roberto, a Spaniard living in Belgium, who considered himself a Camino expert, still walking with his entourage of older single ladies who seemed to hang on every word he uttered as he lectured his way across Spain. We met Grace from Korea, not seen for three weeks. Others included Ken from Saskatoon, France from Ottawa, Marc and his father from Barcelona, and many more familiar faces from the trail. By hook or by crook or by walking sticks, most of us had made it. The many Europeans we met who were doing their Camino in stages would have to wait. I can't imagine that either the passion or the satisfaction from that fragmented approach is as emotional as it is doing the complete walk in one stretch. By far, the most moving reunion was with Kathy and Teresa. We had started out together and now all of us had done it. Since they arrived a few hours after us, we didn't actually see them until the next morning when we arranged to have dinner with them.

However, that afternoon we had things to do so we left the cathedral after a short tour inside. I had only made two reservations for the trip beforehand: the one night in Orisson and then three nights in Santiago, which were at the Hostal La Salle, something between an albergue and a hotel. It took us a while to locate it, but it was relatively close to the downtown. We were pleased with our room, which had four beds—and even more so because the other two would remain unoccupied.

Our black bag had arrived. After dumping our backpacks, we were free to roam unencumbered. That felt liberating. My pack was light, but after five weeks it had become an integral part of me. Our next stop was very important. We headed off to the Pilgrim's Office to collect our Compostela, the reward for our efforts, the certification that we had, in fact, walked every step of the Way. We had faithfully carried our passports, our *credencial del peregrino*, taking care not to lose them. Religiously getting them stamped at every café, every albergue, every restaurant, making sure we had at least three stamps a day. This was the proof that we qualified for a Compostela.

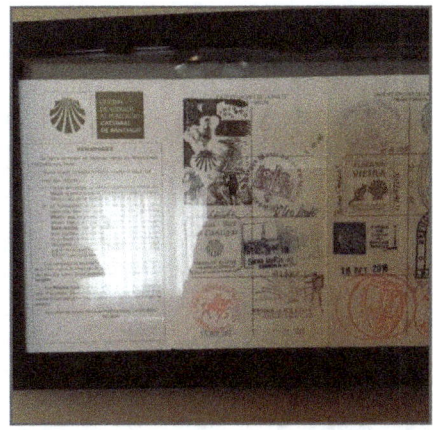 

The clerks were quite meticulous, examining our stamps carefully before confirming that we qualified. We received the basic Compostela, written in Latin, which people could get for walking just from Sarria. Too easy! But for three additional euros we received a second certificate in Spanish that confirmed the total distance we walked and our point of origin as Saint-Jean-Pied-de-Port. That was the most meaningful. Both documents look quite official and now hang with great pride on my office wall.

As we arrived, we met Francisco, whom I hadn't seen for two days. We had our last conversation as we stood in line waiting to apply for our documents. He received the basic Compostela; but given his recent hip replacement, his was well deserved. As we left the office, our rewards in hand, we said our goodbyes. He was heading back to Barcelona the next day. Nice man. I think of him often, and I do watch for news about Catalonia's quest for separation with the added interest of knowing his wish.

Our next decision was whether to attend Mass in the cathedral, which included the ceremony of the Botafumeiro. In October 2016, this only took place on Tuesdays and Fridays. It was a Friday. Jacob was all-in. We decided to go, how could we not? After all, this was the traditional end to the pilgrimage.

53
THE BOTAFUMEIRO

The customary pilgrim's Mass is a stunningly beautiful ceremony highlighted by the unique presentation of the Botafumeiro, a ritual of welcome that goes back almost a thousand years. An integral part of the Mass, the Botafumeiro is one of the most popular symbols of the Camino, an ornate vessel that the monks swing by rope, sending it flying over the cathedral from end to end spewing out incense in the process. As I've mentioned, I am not religious and thus totally unfamiliar with the liturgy of the Roman Catholic Church. That was the norm: only thirty percent of modern pilgrims admit walking the Way for religious reasons. But the cathedral was jam-packed that evening, standing room only. We had entered the Camino for personal reasons, not religious, not even spiritual. By the way, what exactly is spiritual? Does the meaning lie somewhere between mystical and holy? Does it mean religious but not very religious? That's a debate for another day.

Whatever it means, as I sat in the cathedral listening to the service, not understanding a word, watching the eight monks lifting the Botafumeiro up to great heights and swinging it to cover the entire congregation from end to end as it dispersed incense, I knew that my Camino had changed me. No sudden revelation happened. No conversion followed. But my mindset had been altered. My values had as well. My relationship with Jacob had flourished.

Almost everyone who walks the Camino will tell you that it changed them. Maybe just in minor ways. Maybe not for long. Six weeks of a very different lifestyle gives everyone a chance to evaluate where they live and how they live. That's why so many people return again, and some return again and again, trying to recapture the feelings they relished because they do fade over time.

I suppose my heightened sense of history impacted me standing there in a place where people have been having similar feelings, seeing a version of the same ceremony, after completing their own personal pilgrimage, for hundreds of years. The irony of the Botafumeiro part of the service, which is definitely stunning to watch, is that the original purpose was not to provide a greeting or even a celebration of arrival. Nor was it introduced to the glory of God. The practical origin of this delightfully unique ceremony lies in the incense that this elaborate vessel disperses across this huge sanctuary. Those medieval pilgrims did not have convenient albergues with showers readily available. They arrived from all over Europe having taken much longer, more onerous routes and much more time to complete their journey. Those weary travellers were religious and immediately assembled at the cathedral to give thanks to God for their safe travels. They were often filthy, always dirty, and they quite simply stank. The incense was essential to mask their smell and to prevent the spread of any diseases that had developed on the Way. Necessity is the mother of invention. The results often supersede the need, in this case by a huge degree.

To get a real appreciation of what we saw, I suggest you watch a video of the Botafumeiro service on YouTube or watch the movie *The Way*, which also portrays the ceremony. That said, the video doesn't do justice to actually being there. The whole experience was an upper. When the service was over, we joined some fellow travellers for a celebratory dinner arranged as we left the cathedral. There were ten of us, but none were our closest associates. In fact, four of them were Irish friends, all businessmen, whom we hadn't met before. They were quite taken by the fact that I'd written three books on entrepreneurship. I realized that this was something I hadn't mentioned to anyone through the entire trip. Just another aspect of that *other* life that needn't be mentioned along the Way. One of them wrote down the titles, pledging to buy them when he got home. I didn't notice a spike in sales afterwards so I'm not sure if he followed through. To Jacob, my being a published author was nothing new, but he was interested, that perfect strangers showed interest. Each of us were seeing the other in a different light after the past six weeks. Everyone was in a great mood, blown away by the Mass, but we were eating later than usual, no doubt running on adrenalin and more than a little fatigued. The food was very good, but the dinner itself was not particularly eventful. I think all of us were a little stunned to be finished and that was reflected in the muted conversations. The real star of the day had been the cathedral and the Mass.

54
FINALLY, A DAY OF REST

There was a strange feeling the next morning. No early risers woke us up as they tried to get out ahead of the crowd. The lights had not been turned off at 10:00 p.m. the night before. We did not eat breakfast at 7:30 or 8:30 or even 9:30 a.m. There were no paper mattresses or pillow covers to roll up and throw out. The only people in the room were Jacob and me. The black bag was sitting in the corner largely empty and was not on the way to the next destination. Laundry could be done at our leisure and needed to be because we'd been pretty lax about washing our clothes over the past week or so. Maybe we did need that overspray of incense? The morning felt surreal, like we'd been jerked out of our routine rather than simply returning to normal.

We actually skipped breakfast that morning, opting to have a nice lunch instead. I have little memory of that adjustment day. We made plans to meet Kathy and Teresa for dinner. Kathy was feeling much better, no doubt buoyed by persevering to finish when her outcome was in doubt. Jacob and I explored the streets of Santiago, taking our time and looking for souvenirs. I bought a sweatshirt and a T-shirt that I don't wear often, a clamshell with The Cross of Saint James on it, and a small figure of a Templar knight for my military collection. I don't even remember what Jacob bought. It was a stretch to buy anything. We weren't enthralled with this commercial side of the Camino. It was the antithesis of our journey and smacked of tourism in contrast to the benevolent nature of the past six weeks. It was understandable that people wanted to capitalize on the success of El Camino, but it just seemed a little crass. All of these feelings were a manifestation of the mystic of the Way.

By far, the high point of that day was the dinner. We had so much to talk about after being in the same boat for so long. And we had a surprise guest. Our group had set out together from Saint-Jean-Pied-de-Port: Jacob, me, Teresa, Kathy and Richard, who was from California. Richard had struggled that first day, lagging behind the rest of us. Jacob had even dropped back to encourage him and help him finish that shorter walk. He had been at the communal dinner in Orisson and was still sleeping when we'd left. On the second day, while Jacob and I arrived around noon hour, he had straggled in much later by himself. We hadn't seen him since and wondered if he'd dropped far behind or even stopped altogether. We underestimated him. He arrived just twenty-four hours later than us and there he was, sitting at the table with Teresa and Kathy. His presence added to the reunion and provided an answer to the "Whatever happened to…" question that might have puzzled me for years to come.

The conversation was animated. Richard updated us on his challenges over the course of the past five weeks. He hadn't taken a complete day off, as we had. The food was excellent. Jacob's plans for Australia continued to evolve. We carried on well beyond the norm because none of us wanted to call it a day. The night ended with hugs, some near-tears, and the inevitable goodbyes. Jacob would see Teresa and Kathy again in less than two months. As for me, memories of times shared live on vividly and have been richly restored by writing this memoir.

55
MUXÍA AND FINISTERRE

Some pilgrims extend their Camino by walking three more days out to Finisterre, the point the Romans labelled "Land's End." The additional distance is optional and is not officially part of the Camino. The Way ends at the cathedral in Santiago. If you have seen the movie The Way, you'll remember that Martin Sheen's character decides to make that extra walk, along with his Camino friends, to throw his son's ashes into the Atlantic. On his arrival, you see the waves crashing in over the rocks as he tries to spread the ashes. That scene was actually filmed in Muxía, about thirty kilometres from Finisterre. We didn't have time to make the extra trek. Like many fatigued peregrinos, we took a final tour to both, catching the bus out to the area leaving at 9:00 a.m. The only sacrifice was not sleeping in for a second day.

As we got on the tour bus, which was about half full, we found an unexpected surprise. Another reunion: the French lady, Ovietta, was sitting there. Both of us had been sure that she'd dropped out and gone home to France. She'd arrived in Santiago a full day after us, taking four days to do what we had done in three. We were flying to Barcelona the next day and probably would fly over her as she finally returned home. The drive out to Muxía took about an hour, which we spent part of talking with her. She reminded me of my preoccupation with Edith Piaf's "La Vie en Rose," which seemed to please her.

When we reached Muxía, the bus took us out to the point of the peninsula. I think our guide mumbled something about legend saying this was where the body of St. James arrived in Spain, met by the Virgin Mary. All the other passengers stayed up by the sanctuary where the bus had stopped, maybe a hundred metres from the crashing waves. Jacob had other ideas. He wanted to get in the water so he could say he had been in on the eastern shore of the Atlantic. He had plans to go to Nova Scotia the next summer so he could do the same on the western shore. He was also about to leave for Perth in Australia and later New Zealand. On that trip he planned to swim in both the Indian and Pacific Oceans and maybe the Tasman Sea, as well. This was not an opportunity to be missed.

The guide had already confirmed that this was the place where Martin Sheen's character had spread his son's ashes. Just as in the movie, the waves came crashing in, smashing on the rocks. It was pretty wild. Jacob was not fazed. The two of us walked out on the far reach of the point, down close to the waves. This was crazy. He'd be in wet clothes all day. I was charged to take his phone and take enough pictures to verify this achievement. Believe me, those waves were coming in hard. He slipped off his shirt and long pants, revealing that he had shorts on underneath. Then he worked his way down into the water while I watched close by. I took lots of shots. Jake was determined. After a few missteps he got in. It was bloody cold. Another accomplishment during a trip of many. When we got back to the bus, he went into the washroom in the building, returning with his shorts in hand presumably going commando the rest of the way. The other passengers had been watching with interest and congratulated him. Not sure if I heard the Spanish guide whisper,

"Loco" under his breath. I'm sure he was thinking it.

The ride over to Finisterre is shorter, just over half an hour. The first stop was out at the end of the point of the peninsula where the lighthouse stands. This is the place where the Romans believed land ended and water took over in a world they conceived of as flat. The harbour, lower down, is an alternative landing place for St. James in the legend. The farthest point is quite high above the ocean. It was my turn to have a purpose. I had forgotten my Muskoka stone when we approached the Cruz de Ferro, but I had it with me that day. We climbed out as far as possible and I threw my stone from home as far as I could. I'm pretty confident that it made it into the water. A little late but I was finally unburdened, at least symbolically. Any potential burdens waiting at home were forgotten in that uplifting moment.

After that effort we drove down into the harbour, which is quite beautiful and has a few charming seafood restaurants to choose from. We picked one with a lovely view where I had the most delicious shrimp dish and Jacob chose a repeat of his octopus adventure. Overall, we had a great day, having reverted to being tourists with no worries to hamper us. When we got back, there was no need for dinner so we returned to the hotel and packed for our morning flight. I was ready to go home. As for Jacob, Australia was on his mind.

OUR LAST WEEK ON THE TRAIL

56
LOS TEMPLARIOS

Packing that last night went quickly. As I was wrapping up my few souvenirs, including my small Templar knight, I wondered why so many shops along the Way were selling these figures as symbols of El Camino. I knew that the Templars were a French military group best known for two things. One was their role in the Crusades, including their defence of Jerusalem when the Crusaders controlled it. The second was that around 1307, the Pope accused them of heresy, stole their wealth (which was substantial), and ordered all of them arrested and executed. The legend has it that the order was carried out in one day, supposedly on Friday, October 13, 1307. Arrests were made, survivors were tortured to confess, and all of their assets were confiscated. Evidence does not exactly support this version of their destruction happening in a single day but the rest is accurate. In modern times, the impending approach of any Friday the 13th is considered concerning for bad luck. Neither of these facts explained their popularity in Spain.

It turns out that for many years the knights were also charged with protecting the pilgrims travelling to Jerusalem and to Santiago de Compostela, a destination in its own right as well as the only alternative when Jerusalem was controlled by the Moors. The Templars were the guardians of the Way. This may well be where the expression "castles in

Spain" came from as the group had several such castles and we walked close by at least two. However, reading on I found out that the grander castles tend to be in the south.

By this time, Jacob was on an extended video call with his girlfriend in Australia. With nothing else to do, I explored a little more of Spanish history. I was familiar with the Peninsula War and Arthur Wellesley's role (later the Duke of Wellington), and I knew that Spain was an important province of the Roman Empire. I was also aware that the Moors had conquered parts of the country. I didn't know that the Moors surged through and took most of Spain right up to the Basque region around 711 and that they remained in Spain right up to 1492, ironically the year that Columbus sailed to the New World. The fortunes of a united Spain were about to change after almost eight hundred years of occupation, with numerous battles ensuing and territory being ceded back and forth. The Inquisition conducted under Ferdinand and Isabella was directed at both Jews and Muslims. I learned that El Cid was a Castilian knight who fought for both Christian and Muslim armies and grew up near Burgos, which we had walked through. El Cid played a significant part in the early period known as the Reconquista, although he died in 1099, almost three hundred years before the Moors were finally driven out. I learned that Isabella was Queen of Castile and Léon, another area that we'd walked through, before she married Ferdinand II of Aragon and before they financed Columbus on his first voyage.

These few facts are just a small smattering of the long and interesting history of the country we'd just traversed. I do love history and I wished I'd taken more time to read the local chronicles before walking but it's never too late. Brierley does an excellent job of describing virtually every surviving building of historical significance in the villages, towns, and cities. The majority are churches, which I ignored too often when my focus each night was on the distance to be travelled, the terrain to be crossed, the elevations to be climbed, the location of all the cafés and albergues, and nothing more. That was all I could digest in my nighttime reading before sleep took over. In the midst of completing our story, I have read in more detail all of the elements of Mr. Brierley. He made such a contribution to the success and the enjoyment of the modern Camino. Rest in peace, John, content in the knowledge that you have helped hundreds and thousands of would-be pilgrims travel and survive a unique experience tied to the colourful history of this matchless European country. Together, we have walked in the shoes of giants.

57
SEOUL MATES

Earlier I described the intimate nature of the Camino: the social side. After finishing I determined that we had engaged in meaningful conversations and debates with interesting people from twenty-nine countries, six continents, seven Canadian provinces, and fifteen American states, plus the District of Columbia. Diversity is alive and well on the path to Santiago de Compostela. We walked those one million plus steps, roughly thirty thousand a day for thirty-six days, through some challenging terrain. Jacob and I spent over a thousand hours together on our trip in harmony, with no significant dispute.

There was one oddity in our various interactions that persisted throughout: we had zero conversations with the Korean contingent, with the exception of Grace, who spoke English. She was funny and quirky, starting off as a normal walker by herself, never with her fellow Koreans, and later passing us on a bicycle before finally meeting up in Santiago de Compostela. We never actually walked with her. She just kept reappearing out of nowhere when we least expected to see her again. Always a breath of fresh air. We had dinner with her one night. She definitely qualified as one of the Camino "memorables" we met. We loved her. Her choice to walk the Camino alone was a pure whim, a break from university. She was atypical, a free spirit. Also, I suppose she was simply more westernized than her Korean counterparts.

A significant number of her compatriots moved with us throughout our trek. Without fail they seemed a serious bunch, very different than our exuberant Grace. I've been to Korea on business and know that Koreans can be quite stoic. No words were ever exchanged. They did not appear to speak English or Spanish, often using hand gestures to express themselves outside their group. They never appeared to complain. I have no idea why so many South Koreans are attracted to walk in Spain. Regardless, we walked together, often in tandem, but keeping within our own groups. We stayed in the same albergues many times. We nodded to each other politely, well aware that we were struggling with the same issues of fatigue and blisters. Smiles were shared regularly.

Our Korean group liked to get up at 5:00 a.m. for an early start together, just shadows in the dark, so we seldom saw them during the day. These kind and polite people appeared to dress for winter even on the hot days. They much preferred to eat in, which was possible because most albergues have a kitchen. Almost no one else used them. I think part of that was the food they preferred, which was not available on the *peregrino* menus. I never saw any member of their group in a restaurant.

We saw these Koreans most days. They were the silent part of our Camino, but still a part. I do apologize if we played a role in the disappearance of the one lady who chose the wrong fork in the road (I'm just kidding—I'm quite sure she reappeared but I do wonder how far she got that day). Most of all, I want to acknowledge this group with whom we shared the memorable trail for five weeks. I don't know your names or the cities or towns you came from. You don't know mine. But it was a pleasure walking along with you. "Buen Camino" to my Camino Seoul Mates.

58
CREATURES OF THE CAMINO

Once you've completed the task, one tends to repeatedly review the experience and reflect on things you've observed. The Camino is a fluid, ongoing happening with an ever-changing cast of characters—or should I say, in this case, people with distinctive attributes?

First, there are the basic walkers. I think that's where I belonged, those who can average twenty to twenty-five kilometres per day under a wide range of conditions—varying terrain, changing weather, different food, and so on—day after day. That pace allows this type to soak up the countryside and take in some of the many historical sites. They complete their Camino in thirty-three to thirty-six days.

Then there are the racers, who want to prove how fast they can cover the eight hundred kilometres. To them it's all about speed. They pay little attention to their surroundings and shoot for an average rate of forty kilometres per day, covering the complete distance in twenty days. Most of these are young men out to prove a point. Ralph, at seventy-eight, was way outside the curve.

Next come the pacers, who walk more slowly, targeting fifteen to eighteen kilometres per day, and take several days off, extending their journey to fifty days or more. Some pacers are Europeans who are completing a section every year until they finish.

The next level brings us to my friends the cyclists, who leisurely match the pace of the racers while intimidating both the basic walkers and the pacers in the process. And finally, we have the bus people. Occasional walkers who stay in hotels, sleep in, have a relaxing full breakfast, bus partway, then walk a token few kilometres before reboarding the bus to move on to their next hotel. Presumably they pick up enough stamps to get a Compostela, which will be arranged for by their tour manager. No need for them to deal with the crowded Pilgrim's Office. If you're one of those tourists, congratulations for getting an overview of the Camino. If you're reading this: now you know what you missed.

A few other things stood out as we travelled the trail, including a unicyclist; parents pushing their baby in a special stroller; a dog pulling a luggage cart while its pilgrim dog lover walked behind; and a donkey walking with its owner, just to name some. There are people of all stripes: the religious, the masochists, the single ladies, the couples, the old and the young, the early risers, the last to bed, multiple nationalities. The Camino is a rainbow connection, a sweeping mosaic of irregular shapes, sizes, and colours.

59
THE ANTI-CLIMAX

We left Santiago de Compostela mid-morning. Ironically, it took about forty-five minutes to fly over the area that we had walked. When we booked the trip and decided to fly Aer Lingus to Dublin then Barcelona, we planned to spend our last day there before coming home. Barcelona is an interesting city and Francisco had given me a list of must-see places.

We didn't see any of them. The air was out of the balloon for both of us. There was zero interest to tour around, no matter how grand the city was. The flight in was smooth and our transition to our hotel by limo was quick and easy. We checked into our hotel, which had a very comfortable room, looked at each other, and shrugged our shoulders at the same time. It was immediately agreed. We relaxed in the room, eating both lunch and dinner in the dining room. I knew that Jacob was thinking about his next trip. I was just as eager to get home and was regretting that we hadn't booked a direct flight. One last call to Karin and I was set. While Jacob was planning out his four-month trip to Australia and New Zealand, I was busy listing out a long series of anecdotes to be included in my book. Most of them made the cut.

At the time, I felt very much in limbo, one foot still squarely in the Camino and one foot raised to step out. The former had me wondering what to do, the latter what to expect. My routine was broken. My outlook had changed. Meanwhile, Jacob was jumping into the next adventure with both feet. The age difference was at work, but it was more than that.

My goal from day one was to build an unbreakable bond. With our thousand-plus hours together coming to an end, that's one thing we did discuss. Jacob made it clear that my mission had been accomplished. This had been far more than a great trip. It was a once-in-a-lifetime experience. His words, not mine, and music to my ears. That enduring bond is the goal Karin and I have with our children and our grandchildren. It can be reached in different ways. Every Camino is different and every child is different. The foundation for such a bond is inherent in the natural loving relationship that exists from birth and the protective instinct we have for our children and their children. All of these feelings were flooding through my mind as the day in Barcelona faded away and our trip together with it.

Reality was waiting. The next day was a typical full-travel day. Shuttle to the airport. Flight to Dublin. Short layover. Flight to Toronto. Then the last ride, the limo home. The sign on the lawn said "Congratulations!" My doting grandson was about to leave, but the love of my life was smiling and waiting. "Mixed blessings" is an overstatement of how I felt, but this was more than a fair trade. As for Jacob and me, the bond that we built in those six weeks has held strong ever since.

60
HOME AT LAST

Let the celebrations begin. The first days at home were a whirlwind. Returning to the domestic pace on day one, the number of complications, disruptions, requirements, and expectations reverted to the old normal. It felt like I was drawn back into a pressure pot.

It really wasn't much pressure at all, though—it just seemed that way when contrasted with the simplicity of the past six weeks. Our next-door neighbours Grace and Freeman had been tracking our progress and looking out for Karin for the entire time. My second day at home, they hosted a heartwarming "welcome back" party. In the middle of their dining room table was a six-foot-long carrot cake simulating our path on the Camino, with plastic rocks and trees along the Way and flags showing place names. Very supportive, as always. There were about thirty party-goers so I set up a computer slide show of the hundreds of photographs taken by Jacob. Later on, I answered quite a few questions about my trip. It was a moving reception, with which I was delighted but also a little overwhelmed.

A few days later an unbelievable coincidence happened. Almost too unlikely to happen. It was the morning of my seventy-first birthday. Freeman and Grace invited Karin and me out for a celebratory dinner. Still a little unsettled, I suggested we go out for breakfast. By that time, my inner political junkie had been awakened and I was fully expecting Hillary Clinton to win the election, which was the next day. This was a Monday so our favourite breakfast place was closed, which meant going to a different restaurant that we didn't frequent. Everyone suggested I should sleep in so we agreed to go around 10:30 a.m. We were in a place that we never went to at a time that was not normal for breakfast. This is where the story gets weird beyond belief, but I have five witnesses who can corroborate what happened.

I was telling the others about our first communal dinner in Orisson and had just uttered the words "We actually met a couple there from Peterborough whose names were the same as ours, Fred and Karen." As I said the words, I looked up and there they were, that same couple walking toward me, the same Fred and Karen I had said goodbye to in Santiago de Compostela a week before. How could they possibly be in Guelph, more than two hundred miles from their home at exactly the same day and time that we were at that same place, which was an unlikely place for us to be. This is the kind of thing you see in a movie and say, "That could never happen." Karma? Kismet? Predestination? Who knows. There is no logical explanation. We had never discussed that they had a tie to the Guelph area. It turned out that their daughter lived nearby and this was the first time they'd seen her since returning home and on a Monday no less. Easy to believe that the forces of the Camino were at work. Anyway, my good friends at home got to meet two of my compatriots from Spain and hear their version of how we met. Of course, they asked how Jacob was and I confirmed that he had left for Australia two days before. What a world. I still think the whole event is just plain nuts, but how do you explain the inexplicable?

Besides my Compostela and the second Spanish certificate, I arrived home with another badge of honour that I intended to keep for a while: an unkempt six-week beard. My Karin wasn't crazy about it. A couple of days after we got back, we went to see my brother, who was a very bright guy, sadly in the early stages of dementia, a terrible curse. He looked at me questioningly for a moment. Then reached out and touched my beard and said, "Why would you want to grow that thing?" That broke every one up, damaged my ego a bit, but then we had a nice visit.

It was great to be home but a part of me hadn't quite arrived yet.

61
STOP THE WORLD, I WANT TO GET OFF

Those first weeks back, the world seemed upside down. The first night after a beautiful home-cooked meal, I settled down to watch game seven of the World Series. Against all odds, the Chicago Cubs—perennial losers, who had been down three games to one, and had to play games six and seven away from home in Cleveland—won that night in extra innings to claim the World Series title. Unheard of! They hadn't won the World Series since 1908, a hundred and eight years before.

The next night I sat down to watch the American election, where Hillary Clinton was up in the polls by five points and was fully expected to win. So much of the normal election process had occurred in those six weeks we were way, we had no idea of all the oddities that had taken place. I didn't have much respect for Trump, well known to be a failed businessman who had created a misleading image of himself through reality TV. Our version of "The Eve of Destruction" was echoing in my mind. The pipedream of a Hillary victory disappeared quickly as Trump took an early lead that he didn't relinquish.

Two nights staying up late to watch events that had unlikely outcomes. Then we had the incident when Fred and Karen showed up at breakfast. Weird things were happening. The world seemed to be a little murky, clearly out of focus. Things were so off base that I began to dream that after fifty years, just maybe, the Toronto Maple Leafs could win the Stanley Cup. Things do happen in threes, but the playoffs were months way. Their record almost made them the Cubs of the NHL. When I looked into how the team was doing early in the season, I found a few new names in the line-up, two young guys named Mathews and Marner. Looking deeper, I found that Mathews had scored four goals in his first game. Wow. The pundits were predicting a bright future for the team based on the future of these budding new stars. Surely, the Leafs were on their way to a Cup, maybe more than one. Still waiting for that.

All of these things happening in a short time had me reeling. What was next? I thought I just needed-to readjust and things would normalize, but that wasn't exactly the case.

62
THE CAMINO BLUES

The Camino Blues isn't a song, although it could be. Instead, it's a serious phenomenon that can haunt you for months. At first, I thought it was just me experiencing something like kids feel when they come home from a few weeks at summer camp: a time when they miss their new friends and the reality hits that they might never see them again. But I had been on lots of southern vacations where we met people, feeling a connection but just never following up. We'd also taken a three-week bus tour of Europe with a likeable group of Aussies of whom we almost immediately lost track. Assimilating back to our everyday life had never been an issue. This was different. I gave it my own name—the Camino Blues—only to find out it was a common reaction and the name was anything but new.

This period of listlessness felt like a hangover. My excuse was that I was suffering from grandson withdrawal. That was definitely a factor. Hours of talking about nothing and everything ended abruptly. Frequent emails were exchanged but even those soon slowed as Jacob became immersed in his Australian adventure. Whatever enthusiasm I had was evoked when someone asked me about "The Trip." That happened often enough to give me a temporary lift.

This was clearly irrational. Noise bothered me. The constant chatter on television made me anxious. The thought of a Donald Trump presidency was depressing. Winter was almost here. I loved the tranquility of the Camino, but that was mixed in with an ongoing bonding process from a large support group facing exactly the same challenges. That situation is rare in life. Most of the time you're on your own, either individually or as a family. This reintroduction to my former existence was entirely on my shoulders. I felt disconnected and for lack of a better description indifferent, borderline lethargic, and anything but motivated. All of this was accentuated by the reality that I was ninety percent retired, with no major project on the horizon. This level of melancholy from a guy who wrote a book called *Everyday Entrepreneur—Making it Happen*, a problem-solver and a self-starter. Someone who never misses a deadline. Karin was worried about me. I was worried about me!

We started to search for clues online. Google "the Camino Blues" and you'll find lots of commentary. Initially, the most important thing for me was accepting "You are not alone." From what I could gather, this roller coaster of emotions I was feeling was normal and would end anywhere from two weeks to several months. Apparently, my mind signed on for the extended program because it took me six months. I've talked to Jacob about this and he had no such experience. Mind you, he jumped right into an equally exciting venture, maybe more exciting: touring Australia and New Zealand with a more attractive travelling companion.

Two of the suggestions to dispel the cloud hanging over me were to keep walking and to stay in touch with the Camino family. I joined groups on both Facebook and LinkedIn, which helped a bit. The Christmas season helped a bit. We had video calls with Jacob at Christmas and saw Teresa on the call as well. In January I started to write this book. The overhanging weight of these doldrums definitely caused me to stop writing. However, all of these things collectively helped lift my spirits. Why wasn't the accomplishment enough? I never could pinpoint why I felt like I did or why it persisted so long. My outreach to others who were Camino veterans shed no light on this other than to confirm it was "normal." It didn't feel normal.

I suppose the final ingredient to allow me to bounce back was the period in March and April when we spent time at our condo in Florida.

Jacob came back in March and came to visit us for a few days. This was a major step forward. He was full of exuberance about our trip and his trip and what he was going to do when he got home. By the time we returned to Guelph, spring was on the rise and so was I, but there was no appetite to return to the book. Eight years later, I've now resumed the effort. No more unease, just pure nostalgia as I revisit one of the best times of my life.

As an aside on that Florida trip, I still had my beard. Karin still didn't like it. One day when she was out, I decided to appease her. Maybe shaving off my beard was a concession that I was back. When she returned, we had lunch together and she didn't notice. That afternoon we were playing our weekly game of golf with our friends Howard and Irene, followed by dinner out. During the game, no one noticed that the beard was gone. At dinner, menus came and we ordered and no one noticed. Finally, when our glasses of wine arrived, I proposed a toast "to three of the most unobservant people I know, including my dear wife, who is so enthralled with me that she didn't notice that the last vestige of my Camino disappeared this morning."

63
WHY NOW? THE BLENDED BOOK

As I've mentioned, I started to write this memoir in January 2017, two months after Jacob and I returned to Canada. I finished about forty percent of the manuscript and then just stopped, not sure that I had more to say. Over the past year or so I was asked to speak to PROBUS, a fellowship organization for retirees, sharing my experiences on the Camino. That first presentation led to a second, which forced me to revisit the fall of 2016 in more depth. The process rekindled the memories and awakened feelings that had faded over the years. My journal, long ignored, served its purpose well, triggering so many experiences with clarity. My Camino is back.

The pages from both periods are intermingled. You may or may not recognize the difference in various sections. The earlier effort relied on my extended Camino high, which I rekindled for brief periods as I wrote. The Camino Blues quashed that and I stopped. The anecdotes written more recently are based on a different perspective. Bringing back the memories is only part of the impact. Those delayed words are written from a longer-term perspective. They show that my Camino experience has endured. I don't need to do it again. For me, it was indeed an experience of a lifetime. No need to replicate. Just revisit my journal and my many photographs and reread this memoir. What instantly took me back was reading the forty or so pages I wrote in 2017. That's all it took. Now I get to share my trip with my family, my friends, and with you.

Your Camino doesn't have to be a walk in Spain. I suppose that my Camino was similar to going to a retreat, removing myself from day-to-day life for a short time. If you want to walk, El Camino is still there, more popular than ever. In addition, new and innovative imitators are springing up around the world. Well-defined programs are available in Prince Edward Island and Ireland, to name a couple. You'll find others online. Realistically, you don't even have to walk at all. Daily meditation is a first step. A two-week holiday filled with activity won't work. That's just an extension of the fast-paced world we live in. You really need to step back and step out. All I can suggest to find your own way is to do something that removes you from a life fleeting by, out of control.

As for this story, it's my account, my recollection, my experience, my perceptions, my feelings. To get the complete or other side of the story, you'll have to ask Jacob. As I've said repeatedly, everyone's Camino is different. Walking with your grandfather is completely different than walking with your grandson. I only wish that I'd had the chance to walk with my grandfathers, those two I never knew, even for a day. Oh, the stories they could tell.

64
SUBLIMITY

What is sublimity? It's definitely not a word we use often, if at all. Maybe that's because the word is odd or maybe it's because the concept is rare. The noun sublimity describes a fleeting feeling or characteristic that's hard to define. When a sight or an experience can be described as sublime, it has achieved or is approaching greatness. The Latin root sublimis means "uplifted" or even "exalted." The most common synonyms are glorious, resplendent, amazing, awesome, stunning, and wondrous. In any case, it is a very special feeling.

Sublimity is a feeling you will undoubtedly achieve on your Camino, at least most pilgrims do. This is the ill-defined feeling that attracts many people to do multiple Caminos. I have met a fellow who was planning his twelfth, quite a few others who have done a second, third, or fourth. Why? Is it the fellowship?—a definite phenomenon from a unique shared experience. Is it the sights?—that's subjective, meaning some are great, others not so much. Is it the challenge?—very real but not exactly daunting. Is it the food?—definitely not. So, what is it?

Well, I believe that the sublimity of the Camino is grounded in its simplicity. More specifically, it's an experience that demands a return to the basics. It's like a revolving summer camp that moves from place to place, with camp friends moving in and out of your sphere. Your goals are straightforward: eat, drink, walk; eat, drink, walk; eat, drink, walk; shower, eat, drink, plan, and sleep. Most of that drinking is water and you will never have too much. The wine at the end of the day is a great sleep aid, the short-term cure for blisters, and of course enlivens the nightly conversation. You accomplish daily goals; and at the end of your trek, usually between thirty and forty days, you accomplish your overall goal: you reach Santiago de Compostela. But so does everyone else, at least most of those who started with the commitment to go the full distance of eight hundred kilometres. Worries are few.

When was the last time you had the opportunity to walk through a country? Have you ever even walked through your own for any distance? Do you feel an intimate connection with the countries you've visited for a week, spending much of that week on a tour bus rushing from sight to sight, taking myriads of pictures because otherwise you will have no context or memories of the experience?

The Camino is different. You walk through rural villages, passing by stone houses that have endured through the ages. Areas where El Cid was the hero, where Cesare Borgia died, where the Knights Templar reigned supreme and yet were destroyed, where Wellington's armies pursued those of Napoleon. Passing through centuries-old farms and vineyards, you walk beside cows, horses, and donkeys. This is not exactly a walk in the park, but it is a walk that the average person can do *if* they want to do it.

This experience is so fundamentally different from everyday twenty-first-century society. How does it compare to your own everyday life? When I was walking, I remembered the question that Mahatma Gandhi was once asked: "What do you think of western civilization?" Gandhi is reported to have replied, "I think it would be a good idea." Maybe, but I know that Gandhi meant nothing resembling the fast-paced, self-centred, technology-dominated society that both captivates and enslaves us. That society is the antithesis of sublimity. The Camino is where you will find that feeling and it will stay with you.

So, if you can: JUST DO IT! And if for some reason you've left it too late, strive to find your own personal Camino, whatever that may be. Buen Camino to all.

MORE MEMORIES OF OUR CAMINO

www.ingramcontent.com/pod-product-compliance
Lightning Source LLC
Chambersburg PA
CBHW071916290426
44110CB00013B/1380